The Essentials of
Good Table Service

Y0-BDV-761

SCHOOL OF HOTEL ADMINISTRATION, CORNELL UNIVERSITY, ITHACA, NY

© 1975, *The Cornell Hotel and Restaurant Administration Quarterly*
New printing, 1985— ALL RIGHTS RESERVED
SCHOOL OF HOTEL ADMINISTRATION, CORNELL UNIVERSITY
Statler Hall, Ithaca, NY 14853-0223

(ISBN #0-937056-02-2)

The Essentials of Good Table Service

THE WAITER OR WAITRESS in a high quality restaurant earns far more than does the typical department store clerk or office worker when wages, gratuities, uniforms and meals are counted in. His role is that of merchandising food and of making certain that the people seated at his tables enjoy the dining occasion. Some restaurants call their waiters "hosts" or "hostesses" to promote an attitude of gracious service among the employees.

To most Americans, dining in a fine restaurant is a treat reserved for special occasions. The people seated at your tables may be celebrating an anniversary, entertaining friends or business acquaintances, seeking consolation through food, or merely looking for a change in pace.

You can contribute significantly to the success of the occasion by your manner, appearance, and expert gracious service. For no matter how painstakingly a dish is concocted in the kitchen, it can be ruined for the diner if it is shoved before him by an inexperienced or surly waiter. Since it is the waiter, not the restaurant manager or owner, who serves the customers and talks to them, the waiter can build or lose business for his establishment. Disgruntled customers seldom complain—they simply walk out and do not return.

The well-trained waiter should know the difference between good and poor service, between show and bluff. He should be knowledgeable about American, French, and Russian table service because all three patterns are currently in use in American hotels and restaurants. While no one manner of table service is the only correct one, the waiter should follow the restaurant's established pattern and know when to adapt the pattern to better serve the needs of the guests.

The reader of this manual may be a trainee who plans to become a first-class or professional waiter. Or the reader may be a student or housewife seeking temporary employment to augment family income. Whatever his goal, his earnings and his pride in his work will be greater when he can render expert service.

1. The Headwaiter or Hostess

The principal responsibilities of the headwaiter or hostess in guest relations are to:

- Greet and seat the guests, according to their preferences when tables and waiter schedules permit.
- Supervise and check on service and setups.
- Be impartial and impersonal in his relations with the service staff.
- Intercede between guests and waiters when difficulties arise and report problems that cannot be handled to the manager.
- Perform sundry other duties that vary with the individual establishment.
- As guests leave the dining area, thank them for their patronage, invite them to return — and ascertain if they were pleased with food and service.

It is desirable that the headwaiter or hostess have had experience as a waiter. When this is not the case, he or she should have had thorough training in the basic procedures of table service and have had experience as an assistant to the headwaiter or hostess.

The headwaiter is responsible for the proper setup of tables and chairs before the dining room opens. He should make a tour of the dining room before it opens to check on each setup and on the proper placing of tables and chairs.

It is also the duty of the headwaiter to go over the menu with the waiters before the dining room is opened. He should brief the staff on the meaning of menu terms, which items are ready to be served, and which items require considerable preparation time.

The headwaiter is further responsible for the deportment of the waiters on the floor. Two or three waiters gathering at a station for a chat when the dining room is filled with patrons indicates poor service and lack of supervision. Such visiting can be condoned before the room is officially opened or when there are only a few patrons seated elsewhere in the dining room where they are being well cared for. He should not openly discipline waiters in the dining room.

Demeanor

The headwaiter (or hostess), if not in uniform, should be fashionably but neatly dressed. Alertness, a genuine smile, and poise in giving a cordial greeting are also important. He should learn the names and other pertinent facts about regular patrons — a card index would be helpful — as well as their preferences as to table location, waiters, and other such information. He should be exceedingly careful never to overstep the thin line between "friendliness" and "familiarity." Needless to say, the headwaiter should not smoke, chew gum, nor openly visit with guests or waiters while on the job.

Greeting Guests

The stranger should be greeted with the same cordiality as the regular patron. All guests (with few exceptions) are "friends" of the manager — their patronage is sought; make them feel welcome.

When a man or woman comes in alone, greet him pleasantly, "Good morning (or Good evening), this way please." Don't say, "Just one?" or "Are you alone?" When tables are plentiful, tactfully ask, "Do you prefer a banquette (booth or other desirable location)?"

Hats and wraps should be taken care of as near the entrance as possible. To women, say, "May I help you with your coat?" To men, it is permissible to say, "May I take your hat (and topcoat)?"

Seating Guests

An efficient headwaiter knows what seats are available without having to ask the guest to wait while he looks for a table. The headwaiter, when not engaged in greeting and seating guests, should scan the dining room quickly to check on available tables, the guests' progress in dining, and whether a guest is in need of service. (When a waiter is not immediately available to answer a guest's signal or searching look, then the headwaiter should step up and inquire, "May I be of assistance, sir?" In passing tables *en route* from seating guests, he might ask, "Is everything all right, sir?")

When extra setups and chairs are needed at a table, have these changes made if at all possible before taking the guests to the table. Have unneeded setups also removed from the table and in some instances the extra chairs. Special accommodations for children should be made at this time.

The host should precede guests to their table, carrying menus in his hand, saying, "This way, please." It is conventional to seat women guests facing the dining room, rather than a wall, but the host should be alert to individual preferences in this regard. Similarly, when two couples are dining at a banquette, it is conventional to seat the ladies to face the room unless they prefer another arrangement.

Menus

After the guests are seated, hand them menus. For couples, begin with the lady. For a party, begin with the person to the right of the host and proceed counterclockwise around the table. The host may indicate as soon as his party has been seated that he will order for the entire group. If a menu or two has already been distributed, collect only those handed back voluntarily. When there is no children's menu, it is not advisable to give the regular menu to small children unless their parents so request.

Ushering Out Guests

The saying of "Goodbye—I hope you enjoyed your dinner," to departing guests is as important as greeting them when they first come into the dining room. Assist them with hats and wraps if there is no checkroom service. The headwaiter thus has an opportunity to learn whether the guests enjoyed their meal, whether the service was good, and whether some misunderstanding arose. Good will is engendered when explanations and adjustments are made immediately.

A good rule to follow is "Don't try to put *others* in their place. Put *yourself* in their place."

2.   General Rules for Servers*

The person entering a dining room is embarking upon an important personal mission—one he hopes will be pleasant, refreshing, and satisfying. In fulfilling his hopes, the role of the waiter is paramount. The waiter's interest, courtesy, and skill can do much to insure the guest's enjoyment.

---

*The phrase "waiter" is used through most of the text to refer to members of the service staff, whether male or female. The server's duties in the kitchen and pantry area (layout, pickup, garnishing, and checking out) are not covered in this discussion because the details vary greatly among different operations. The rules for correct table setup are given under "American service," "French service," etc., later in this manual.

New waiters and waitresses should be properly trained. Here a hostess has just completed a lesson in napkin folding and will next proceed to table setting. A "professional" atmosphere was created by having the "students" in uniform.

Lack of interest and skill can make the dining drama a farce and insult the guest's sensibilities. The waiter, therefore, should not approach his duties as menial or servile: he plays a major role in that most appreciated art — gracious dining.

Guest Relations

As the waiter, think of yourself as the party's host, greet the guests pleasantly by name if possible, and give each guest the kind of service he wants:

WHEN — the guest is in a hurry, provide speedy service.

— the guest is lonely, a few friendly words may make his food taste better.

— the menu is "Greek" to him, tell him how the dish is prepared.

— he is celebrating, suggest dishes and wines that will make the meal "an occasion."

— he is budgeting (you can sense this), suggest menu combinations that will enable him to have a fine meal at modest cost — he'll come back when his purse is fatter.

— he is dieting, suggest suitable menu items and offer substitutes for calorie-heavy dressing and sauces.

The basic pattern of your work can be summed up in a few words — make a genuine effort to please the guest. If you were to ask guests what qualities they expect in a good waiter, you'd hear two words repeated again and again — courtesy and understanding. These qualities can be developed by anyone who considers them important. While it is difficult to be pleasant all the time, a "high average" is possible. A smile, a courteous greeting, a polite inquiry are necessary rudiments for success. Genuinely discourteous customers are few. Most people respond to courtesy in others.

Never get into an argument with a guest — call the headwaiter or hostess, who, in turn, may refer matters to the manager. If you should get involved in a lengthy conversation with a guest, especially on a topic you should not discuss, the situation can be solved with a smile, an apology, and a hasty departure.

Use an individual approach with the guests you serve. Some are hungry; some are lonely; and some just plain fussy. Some are strangers in the city and don't know their way around; others are quite knowing and disdain assistance. Some will welcome suggestions for dining while others will assume you are trying to unload yesterday's leftovers.

No matter how varied the situations you encounter, you will soon discover prototypes among guests. Develop an approach to each situation and use a little psychology.

Personal Appearance

Waiters and waitresses in many restaurants are selected and dressed to complement the room's design. As part of the total theme, the staff's trim-fitting uniforms and attractive personal appearance are vitally important. When the staff is in-

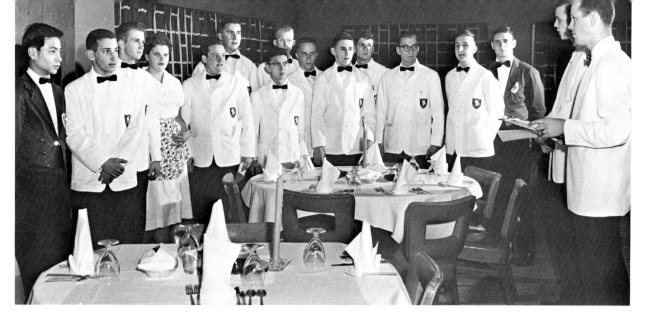

Before the dining room opens, the headwaiter or hostess briefs the service staff on menu offerings and the specific details concerning dishes and their preparation time. The service staff also passes inspection for proper uniform and good grooming.

different to personal grooming, they offend guests, who doubt the cleanliness of everything served. A clean uniform in a locker, for emergencies, with another at the laundry, helps to assure a presentable appearance.

Grooming for both waiters and waitresses should be fastidious. The goal is to present a wholesome, healthy, natural appearance — attractive, clean, no body or mouth odors. Smoking and gum chewing should be taboo while on duty. Politeness, courtesy, helpfulness, and a well-modulated voice are additional virtues.

Waiters' uniforms should be well-tailored and fit them properly. It is likewise important that uniforms be clean, well-pressed, and have no missing buttons. As to grooming, each waiter should be carefully barbered, his hair trimmed to a length which complies with health laws. His hands and fingernails must be scrupulously clean. He should wear conventional, comfortable shoes and socks without holes that match his uniform.

Waitresses should make a special effort to look attractive and wholesome. Today's semi-opaque uniforms of man-made fibers require proper undergarments to avoid the peekaboo look. Hair should be clean and carefully combed. Long hair should either be worn pinned into a chignon or bound back of the shoulders with a barette or a ribbon matching the costume. State sanitary laws typically require hairnets. (Men with beards and long hair may also be required by law to cover them with hairnets!) Make-up should appear "natural" without excessive use of eyeliner, mascara, and lipstick. Fingernails should be shapely, not extending beyond the fingertips, while nail polish should be light in color and never chipped. As for jewelry, a wristwatch and a simple ring should suffice. Shoes should be comfortable and conventional, and hose should have no runs.

Waiters and waitresses, in short, play an essential role in the restaurant's success. Attractive appearance and agreeable personality aid them in developing good relations with the guests they serve. These rules, incidentally, will also assist them to become poised and likeable to all people with whom they associate.

Teamwork

So far, the discussion has hinged on the individual role played by the waiter in the dining room. But the waiter should be cautioned that his is a "supporting role" — the "spotlight" is on the guest. Everyone on the staff is in the "cast" and must work together and come in on cue: headwaiter, waiter, and busboy. When one member of the "cast" is busy serving other guests or is absent for a minute, then other employees should perform whatever part of his role they can as his "stand in." The guest should not be left unattended, ignored, nor made to feel insignificant. When this happens, even for a short time, the waiter's performance is "a flop."

Teamwork makes everyone's job easier. The waiter who is competent in his job understands and appreciates his co-workers' problems. He is quick to see where and how he can help. This willingness to step in when needed is appreciated

5

and insures the waiter the cooperation he needs in giving a smooth performance. Observe these helpful points:

- Report on time, properly dressed for work.
- Do not criticize or pick an argument with anyone.
- Give compliments when and where they are due.
- Don't take the "limelight" away from the waiter assigned to the guest.
- Give help where you can when it is needed but do not get in the way of other people in the working area.

Know Preparation Time

Long delays and lukewarm food can be avoided when the waiter knows in advance the preparation time for each dish. Since the *a la carte* items on the menu remain the same, generally only about six to nine daily selections must be learned for each meal. The headwaiter learns the preparation time from the chef, briefs the service crew on such matters, and also explains menu terms.

Orders from guests can then be placed on a coordinated basis so that dishes can be served to several guests at a table at approximately the same time. When guests at one table order dishes requiring widely different times to prepare, he should tactfully tell them. Some may wish to change their orders for the convenience of the persons with whom they are dining.

When the waiter is not aware of the differences required for preparing dishes, the dish ready first may stand at room temperature until it becomes cold and needs reheating. An oven-hot dinner plate is dangerous both to the waiter and to the guest. Unless the guest is warned, serious burns may occur. Moreover, when the kitchen personnel must reheat dishes, service is slowed for the entire dining room.

Busboy

The busboy should remove unnecessary setups from the table (and sometimes extra chairs) while the guests are being seated. Then he should pour water for the guests, and if cocktails are not ordered, serve them butter from the side stand and offer them bread and rolls. When the busboy is absent, the waiter may need to perform these duties. The busboy should also remove dishes and used (as well as unused extra) silverware when each course is finished.

Taking Orders

After greeting the guest or party host ("Good evening, etc."), the waiter should inquire, "May I bring you a cocktail?" Some guests may wish to see the wine list which should be readily at hand when not incorporated into the menu. The party host may take orders from his guests and relay them to the waiter; or he may indicate that the waiter should take them. When the latter occurs, start with the person to the right of the host and proceed counterclockwise around the table, using a diagram so that the drinks can be served without interrupting conversation.

When the cocktails have been served, inquire, "Would you like to order, sir?" If the host does, the waiter should tactfully learn whether the guests are in a hurry. Then he can judge whether the order should be placed in the kitchen immediately or whether the party will want another round of drinks. Only when guests stress their need for haste should the meal be served while guests still have their cocktail glasses.

Order Sequence. The guest's order should be taken from his left. Begin first with the host, who will then indicate whether he will order for the entire party or whether each guest is to place his own order. When a couple is dining, it is customary to ask the lady's escort for her order unless he otherwise indicates.

When the host of the party indicates that his guests are to give their own orders, begin with the person to the right of the host and proceed counterclockwise around the table.

System for Writing Orders. To provide smooth, inobtrusive service, orders must be systematically taken. Without a definite procedure for doing so, the taking of orders for a group can be confusing. Use memo-pad slips instead of the tinted check or bill form. Guests often change their minds in giving their orders and the memo slip on which you can cross out items prevents ending up with a messy bill.

A good system to follow is mentally to number all the chairs at a table in a set pattern. List one chair at each table as "No. 1", using some benchmark such as a window, the entrance, or other conspicuous object. As you write each guest's order, put these numbers down on the paper. Use as many abbreviations as possible for this speeds up the order taking (*See illustration*).

This system eliminates confusion, making it unnecessary for the waiter to ask, when serving,

AN ABBREVIATION SYSTEM FOR TAKING ORDERS

```
Table 15
 1 S      FM r    C, bp     (Dessert)
 2 Sc     R  m     Cf, ff
 3 S      FM w     Cf, ff
 4 S      F        B, bp
 5 LC     F        B, bp
```

Sc	Shrimp Cocktail	m	medium
LC	Lobster Cocktail	w	well done
S	Soup	C	Carrots
FM	Filet Mignon	Cf	Cauliflower
R	Roast Beef	B	Beans
F	Fish	bp	boiled potatoes
r	rare	ff	french fried potatoes

"Who ordered the fish, please?" This system also makes it possible for one waiter to take orders for this table and another waiter to continue with the service later on. Or, one waiter may take the order while another waiter serves the plates. Dessert orders are ordinarily taken when the main dish has been consumed.

The waiter should not leave the table until he is positive that he has taken the orders correctly. Should there be doubt, repeat the orders in sequence to guard against omissions and other errors. This practice saves extra trips to the kitchen and keeps the guests from impatient waiting. The waiter should bear in mind the different preparation times of the dishes ordered and tactfully inform the guests so they can change their orders if they wish to do so.

Guests' Errors in Ordering

Some guests make mistakes in giving their orders. The waiter should keep alert and listen carefully. Breakfast orders are especially difficult as guests are often sleepy or have their faces buried in newspapers. No matter how wrong the guest may be about his order, do not argue with him. He probably will not touch a dish that he believes he didn't order. Accept extra trips to the kitchen as part of your role and do so cheerfully. Be tactful with the guest, assume responsibility (to the guest at least) for the error, and you are more likely to earn a tip as well as his good will.

Food Merchandising

The waiter may be asked to suggest specialties. Or, if the guest is hesitant in making up his mind, the waiter may make suggestions. These suggestions should be made in a manner that seems helpful rather than "pushing."

"Have you tried our Veal Scaloppine?" (or name another dish) is better than to say, "How about a steak?" Then explain the preparation of dishes if the guest still seems hesitant about ones you mention.

A guest is often influenced by what he sees other diners eating at adjacent tables. Rolling carts for roast beef, salads, and desserts help guests make decisions. Sometimes a waiter will bring in a choice, uncooked steak on a platter to show a party obviously celebrating an occasion. The serving of a wine bottle in a wine stand by the *sommelier* (wine steward) at a nearby table will prompt some groups to order wine. The same is true for flaming desserts.

Joseph Faussone, a famous chef, presents Lobster Thermidor to a guest in the Statler Inn dining room.

(Right) Walter Tode, winner of the International Medal of the Societe Gastronomes Alsace, serves Crepes Suzettes in the Statler Inn dining room. The onlookers in the rear appreciate his showmanship.

Food Merchandising: (*Upper left*) Sommelier (*wine steward*) poses by display of red and white wines and champagne with proper glasses. Grapes, flowers, and seasonal decorations added to this display attract attention in the foyer. (*Above*) Roast beef is carved before a guest from poulette pan on rolling cart. One employee should be trained to carve in public. (*Lower left*) Lobster displayed with garnishes on a platter.

In taking dessert orders, remember the old adage, don't ask "if"; ask "which." Ask, "Which dessert will you have, the parfait or the pumpkin pie with ginger and whipped cream?" Or say, "Wouldn't you like to try our specialty — Statler apple pie made of fresh New York State apples?" When lobster or roast beef is ordered for what is obviously a festive event, suggest a white or red wine to make the dish more eventful. This "soft sell" of good food encourages the guest to enjoy himself — he does have the option of saying "No" — and makes the dinner check larger and encourages better tips.

Carrying a Tray

The food in most American restaurants is brought into the dining room on large trays carried on the left hand. (*See illustration on the next page.*) The left hand is used because doors open to the right and, if there is no electronic opener, must either be pushed open with the right hand or kicked open. If the door is kicked open, it may slam back faster than is expected. When the waiter carries his tray on his right hand, he cannot see the door slamming and his tray may be knocked off his hand.

Basic Rules for Service

These rules are followed in most American restaurants, except when consideration for the guest's comfort dictates otherwise:

- **All food is served from the left.**
- **All beverages are served from the right.**
- **Serve ladies, older persons, and children first; in a group of ladies or a group of men, begin with the person to the *right* of the host and proceed counterclockwise.**
- **Clear dishes from the right.**
- **Do not stack dishes or scrape plates before a guest.**

Accidents

"Gremlins" roost in even the best-run dining rooms. Thus, accidents happen and many of them may not be the waiter's fault. He regularly works with hot dishes and should know how to balance a tray. He should serve all liquids with great care. The waiter should also know how to pivot in narrow places.

The guest does not have these skills. A guest's sudden or careless movement can cause an accident. Even though the waiter is not to blame, every mishap should be his concern. Most restaurants pay the bill when a guest's clothing is stained. The more the waiter knows about removing stains or reducing their unsightliness the more helpful he can be. First offer an expression of regret to soothe the customer's irritation and then take action. It doesn't matter whose job it is to clean up or where the busboy happens to be — the waiter must show concern and be helpful.

Chatting on Duty

Keep your eyes constantly on your customers. During a lull, waiters may engage in limited conversation. But during rush periods they deserve a severe reprimand for doing so especially when guests are being ignored.

Check Stations Constantly

Before disappearing into the kitchen, check your station to see whether guests are trying to get your attention. All of us have seen guests seated at tables (where correct deportment requires them to stay) frantically trying to catch the waiter's attention. The guest breaks up his conversation, ignores his companions, and gazes spellbound at the waiter's disappearing back. An alert waiter does not permit persons at his station to undergo this frustration. When the waiter is serving at another table, it is permissible for him to nod in recognition to a guest's signal. The guest can then relax and resume his conversation, knowing that the waiter will be there in a moment.

Presenting the Check

In most formal dining rooms it is customary to hold the check until the guest asks for it and then to present it face down on a small plate at the guest's left. Otherwise, present the check to the guest when he has finished with his dessert.

Tipping

Restaurateurs know that satisfied guests are their most important asset and displeased guests their greatest liability. Waiters who try to squeeze an extra tip from guests can be responsible for losing business — and thereby decreasing their own earnings.

Thank the guest graciously, even for a small gratuity. It is not in keeping with the American tradition of self-respect for a waiter to haggle over a tip. Retail store clerks and bank tellers receive no gratuities; yet, they are unfailingly courteous in thanking the patron and inviting him to come back. Is the waiter's job more servile than their positions in serving the public?

Guest Comments

The waiter should mentally record guest reactions to the service, food, comfort, and atmosphere of the dining room. This information has value. Remarks made to a waiter, or within his hearing, should be written down and sent to the kitchen or via the headwaiter to the management. A guest's praise should be sent along as well as his complaints.

Carrying a Tray: (*Left*) Tray is balanced on palm of hand. Heavy trays can rest on shoulder. (*Center*) Balance tray with other hand before setting on stand. (*Right*) Some male waiters learn to balance trays on fingertips, permitting them to swivel through narrow passages in crowded dining rooms.

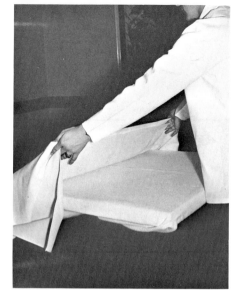

1. Correct way to spread a tablecloth.

2. Tablecloth should touch chair's edge.

3. American Service

In "American service" food is plated in the kitchen and placed before the diner. Side dishes are those for bread and butter and for salad. Coffee is often served with the meal. The general rule is to *"serve solids from the left, liquids from the right, and to remove soiled tableware from the right."* Service is fast, as one waiter can serve many guests, and a minimum of waiter training is needed.

Important to American service is the waiters' service station. These units should be strategically placed to save waiters steps. Sometimes they are located in a screened decorative unit; in other instances they are positioned to service a specific section. Before the dining area opens, these stations should be fully supplied with tableware, napkins, ashtrays, table covers, etc. Pitchers of ice water, trays of iced butter pats and relishes, condiments, the coffee warmers and bun warmers should also be made ready. Tray stands are set up around the room. Periodically, all of these service stations are checked for replenishment by the staff.

Setting the Table

PLACE

1. A "silencer" cloth (piece of felt or foam rubber) on the bare table.
2. A clean tablecloth over the "silencer" pad. (*See Illustration 1, this page.*) When the tablecloth has a crest, make sure that it faces the correct direction. The tablecloth should extend at least 12 inches over the table's edge but should not interfere with the guests' comfort when they are seated. (*See Illustration 2.*)

   (Some restaurants put a "top cloth" over the tablecloth and change only the top when the guest leaves. Before completely stripping a table for resetting, the waiter should always obtain a clean tablecloth from the linen room.)

3. A sugar bowl, salt and pepper shakers, and an ashtray on the table for each two guests. (For tables of more than six, service for every three persons may be sufficient.)

3. The "American cover."

4. Carrying glasses without a tray.

5. Placing goblet on table. ("Frenc cover.")

6. Carrying clean silverware.

7. Holding plate to avoid finger marks.

4. The "covers" — each guest's plate, silverware, glass, and napkin — on the table. *(See Illustration 3.)*

- a folded napkin in the center of the cover and 1/4-in. from the table edge.

- two dinner forks to the *left* of the napkin (all silverware is placed 1/4-in. from the table edge).

- a dinner knife, a bread-and-butter knife (both cutting edges facing the plate) and two teaspoons to the *right* of the napkin in 1, 2, 3, 4 order.

- the bread-and-butter plate at least 1-in. above the fork tines. (An alternate position for the butter knife is to lay it across the top of the bread-and-butter plate parallel to the table edge.)

- the water, glass (bottom up) slightly to the right of the tip of the dinner knife.

The foregoing setup places all silverware needed by the guest (except soup or appetizer with which essential silver is served) on the table ahead of time. "Used" silverware is removed with the plates after the course is completed. The water glass is turned over and filled with ice water as soon as the guest is seated. The only extra attention required is to brush crumbs from the table before serving dessert.

8. American service is from the left.

9. **To Remove Plates: The waiter picks up each plate with his right hand from the guest's right. Out of view, he quietly scrapes food from this plate to the first one removed, shuffling the new plate to the bottom of the stack held with his left hand. Silverware, held in his fingers until all the plates are removed, is laid across the top plate with food scraps.**

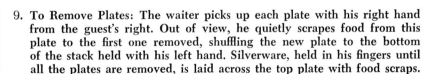

American Service

These basic rules should be memorized:

- All food is served from the guest's left with the *left* hand.
- All beverages are served from the guest's right with the *right* hand.
- Clear dishes from the guest's right.

(The rules above may be modified for the guest's comfort when he is seated in a corner or in a booth.)

Seating the Guest:

- Seat the guest when he enters the dining room. (Many find their own tables.) Remove extra covers from his table.
- Hand him a menu. Pour ice water in his glass (after turning it up) from the guest's right, using the *right hand*.
- Ask him if he wishes a cocktail.
- While the waiter picks up the cocktail at the bar, the guest studies the menu and makes his meal selection.

Taking the Order:

- The waiter returns with the cocktail, serving it from the guest's right.
- The waiter now takes the guest's order.
- The waiter serves the guest bread and butter from the guest's left.
- The waiter takes the guest's order to the kitchen, unless there are indications that the guest will have a second cocktail, and his dinner might grow cold while he enjoys it.

Table Service:

- Soup or an appetizer (and usually the salad) is brought in on a tray from the kitchen. The guest's cocktail glass is removed from the right. The soup spoon or appetizer fork is generally laid either on the right side of the underliner or is placed to the

"cover" right, inside the No. 2 teaspoon. (Never serve the soup or appetizer while the guest is enjoying his cocktail unless he emphasizes that he is in a hurry.)

- The main course (meat and vegetables) is picked up on a plate by the waiter from the kitchen range, ready to serve, and carried in on a tray. The tray is set on a service stand near the guest.
- The soup or appetizer dishes are removed from the right. The main course is served from the guest's left. He is served more butter and offered bread from his left. The guest's water glass is replenished from the right. (*See Illustration 8.*)
- If the guest ordered "coffee with," he is served coffee from his right (*waiter's right hand*).°

Dessert:

- When the guest indicates that he has finished with his main course — keep an eye on him to see whether he needs additional service meanwhile — bring him a dessert menu.
- Remove dishes from the main course from the guest's right (*waiter's right hand*). Replenish water glass from the guest's right. Brush crumbs from the table. Take his dessert order. (*See Illustration 9.*)
- The dessert is brought in on a tray and served from the left.
- Coffee is brought in and served from the right.°
- If nothing further is required by the guest, lay his check inobtrusively on the table, face down to his left and near the table's edge.

° To avoid splashing hot coffee on the guest when pouring it at his elbow, place a folded napkin or a small service plate between the guest and the cup.

Formal dinner place setting. The crest of the service plate (upon which the appetizer is later set) should face the guest and the water goblet should be set slightly to the left of the knife tip because of the large plate. The napkin, folded in rectangles, is placed to the left of the forks. When service plates without crests are used, the napkin is sometimes laid in three large pleats across the plate. Bread and butter plates are added when the appetizer and service plates are removed. *Photo taken at Statler Inn, Cornell University.*

Serving Spoon and Fork — This waiter uses a serving spoon and fork to serve chicken pot pie to a guest in a fine dining room. The handles of the spoon and fork rest in the palm of his hand, the base of the fork held on the spoon handle acting as a clamp controlled by the fingers. His first finger is inserted between the fork and spoon to obtain leverage while his third finger supports the spoon. Practice is needed to perfect this service.

KEYED DISPLAY OF TABLE SILVER COMMONLY USED IN FIRST-CLASS RESTAURANTS.

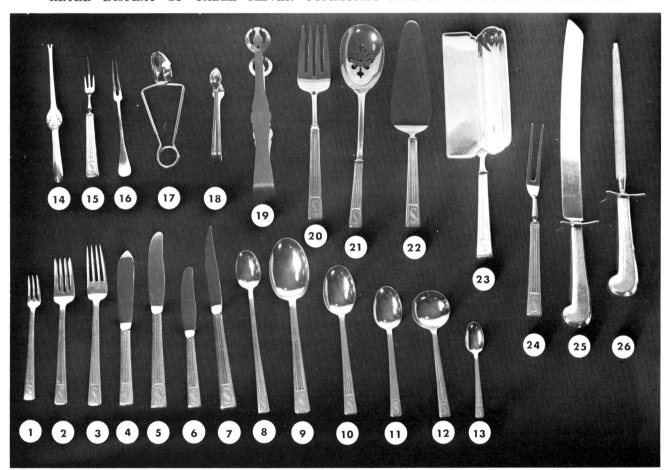

1. Seafood fork
2. Fish fork (often used for salads and desserts)
3. Dinner fork
4. Fish knife
5. Dinner knife
6. Butter knife
7. Steak knife
8. Ice tea or parfait spoon
9. Serving spoon
10. Clear soup spoon
11. Teaspoon
12. Cream soup spoon
13. Demitasse spoon
14. Lobster pick
15. Lobster fork
16. Escargot fork
17. Escargot clamps
18. Sugar tongs
19. Serving or ice tongs
20. Serving fork
21. Slotted serving spoon
22. Cake server
23. Crumber
24–26. Carving set — fork, knife, steel

Silver service place setting. The silver service plate is topped with a doily to cut clatter when the glass underliner and appetizer are set upon it. The napkin, an added ornament, is easy to fold and unfold *(see instructions on page 59)*. The salad fork, placed one inch in from the entrée fork, points to the center of the bread and butter plate, on which the butter knife rests in line with the entrée fork. The goblet, above the tip of the dinner knife, is in line with the center of the bread plate, and between them a dessert fork and spoon are crossed horizontally. *Photo taken at Statler Inn, Cornell University.*

24. "French service" is from the right.

23. A "French cover"

The Four Seasons Restaurant in New York has an exceedingly simple place setting — a black service plate with a center crest, a small ash tray, and an outsize napkin, simply folded. Table linens are color-keyed to the season of the year. Table silver, glassware, and china are brought to the table as each course is served.

The Forum of the Twelve Caesars, also in New York, uses a copper and brass service plate embossed with a head. Other appointments include two forks to the left of the plate and a knife and teaspoon to the right, all heavy silver. Table linens are of heavy gray Belgium linen. This restaurant features chafing dish food and flaming desserts.

English service by a butler and a maid is featured in this New York restaurant. Here a couple is shown enjoying cocktails and hors d'oeuvres. The place setting includes a china service plate (earlier topped with a napkin), a bread and butter plate, and a stemmed water goblet. Two forks are laid to the left of the plate and a dinner knife and teaspoon to the right. The butter knife and a teaspoon are crossed horizontally above the service plate.

A triple-pleated napkin is laid over the china service plate in this Washington, D.C., restaurant. Two forks are placed to the left of the plate and a knife and teaspoon are laid to the right. The butter knife is placed horizontally across the top of the bread and butter plate. Three glasses form a triangle above the point of the dinner knife. Additional silverware may be brought in if the guest orders soup, seafood or fish, or a dessert.

Oriental place settings are simple—a napkin, a fork and a spoon, as shown. Hors d'oeuvres, served with picks, are intended to be eaten with the fingers, after which a rolled damp napkin is presented to the guest. Since Oriental food features slivers of meat and vegetables with rice or noodles, the fork and spoon are usually adequate silverware for Americans.

In Singapore, guests cook slices of meat and vegetables at the table in a Mongolian hot pot filled with broth, using the strainer shown in the place setting. The guest then holds the strainer over his rice bowl and eats food from it with chopsticks. *Singapore photographs, courtesy of Harry Friedman, Miami Beach, Fla.*

Color photograph courtesy of Hospitality Magazine

A Wine Cellar Restaurant

In specialty restaurants, table settings are keyed to the total atmosphere and decor. In the illustration above (a section of Pittypat's Porch Restaurant in Atlanta), a wine cellar atmosphere has been created through open wine bins along one wall, a wine press in the left corner, and an exposed barrel head, partly shown at the upper left.

The oval mahogany table, which seats ten comfortably in bentwood chairs, is left bare to show the rich wood tones. To establish a 19th century motif, silver plates and goblets are used, along with pistol-handled silverware and stemmed wine glasses. Napkins are crisply folded into bishops' hats. Note the fine china pitcher, the silver wine cooler, the "skillet" ashtrays, and the assortment of condiments. Copper candelabra with white tapers and a compote of grapes complete the table setting.

European Hunting Lodge

An elegant masculine note is established by this table setting of the Royal Hunt Room at the Hotel Ambassador in Chicago, which simulates the atmosphere of a European hunting lodge catering to royalty. The central motif of the plates, cups, and glasses is taken from an old English wood carving of a stag's head with antlers. The china is especially designed to be used with black Wedgewood. The tablecloth is of rich damask and the outsized napkins are laid in pleated folds on the left of the service plate.

Restaurant operators who are planning to restyle or upgrade a dining room would do well to study winning table settings displayed in the annual awards contest sponsored by Hospitality Magazine. Other useful ideas can be obtained from the score of other trade publications which include such information. Other good sources are the manufacturers' exhibit.

4. "French" Service

In Europe and England, high-class table service has followed a somewhat similar pattern for several generations. This pattern involves the use of silver serving pieces, the heating and garnishing of food at a side table (or *gueridon*) and the serving of portions to the guests on heated plates either by a waiter, his assistant or sometimes by the host. In its most elaborate form, this service may be called "Service a la Ritz," after Cesar Ritz who founded a line of luxury hotels early in the twentieth century.

The use of this elegant service is declining in America and also in Europe because it requires professionally trained waiters. In earlier decades, a professional waiter's training involved several years' experience coupled with regular classes at a waiters' school before becoming a *commis de rang* — comparable to the regular American waiter. A *commis de rang*, however, was not certified as a professional waiter until he had served a two to three year apprenticeship under a *demi-chef de rang* or a *chef de rang* (professional waiter). Today few young people seek such careers. Even some European schools now teach a modification of French Service resembling Russian Service, described in the next section.

In French service, two waiters usually tend one station. One is called *chef de rang* and the other, *commis de rang*. These two work as a team. Each has his specific duties but helps the other when needed. The duties of the *chef de rang* are:

- Seat the guests if there is no head waiter.
- Take the orders of the guests.
- Serve all drinks.
- Finish the preparation of the food at the table in front of the guests.
- Present the check and collect the money.

The main duties of the *commis* are:
- Receive orders from the *chef de rang*, take them to the kitchen and order the food.
- Pick up the food in the kitchen and bring the food on a tray into the dining room and place it on a side table or cart.
- Serve the plate of food, which the *chef de rang* has prepared at the side table, to the guest.
- Help the *chef de rang* whenever he can.

The French Table Setup

Few people today eat a dinner involving many courses. Generally they consume a meal consisting of soup or an *hors d'oeuvre*, a main course, and a dessert. Consequently, the cover should satisfy these requirements.

PLACE
- an *hors d'oeuvre* plate at the guest "cover" a fraction of an inch from the table's edge. (*See illustration on page 14.*)
- a neatly folded napkin on the *hors d'oeuvre* plate.
- the dinner fork to the *left* of the plate (close to the table's edge).
- the dinner knife to the *right* of the plate with the cutting edge turned toward the plate.
- the soup spoon beside and to the *right* of the dinner knife.
- the butter plate and the butter knife (laid across the plate parallel to the dinner fork) to the *left* of the dinner fork.
- the dessert fork and spoon above the *hors d'oeuvre* plate as these pieces are not used until the dessert is served.
- the water glass (or wineglass) above the tip of the dinner knife.

In French service the glasses are not placed upside-down on the table prior to filling them, because it gives European guests the impression that the dining room is not ready to serve. (When tables are set up an hour or two ahead of serving time, the glasses may be turned upside-down at the cover to prevent dust falling into them; but before the dining room is ready to open the waiter goes around his station turning them right-side-up.)

Since coffee is not served during the dinner, coffee spoons are placed on the table only when needed. Coffee, if served, comes after the dessert. The coffee spoon is placed to the right of the cup and on top of the underliner.

The *Mise en Place*

Mise en place includes all preparations previous to the opening of the dining room. The conscientious waiter has everything ready and at a place easily accessible for the time when it is needed.

Most important is the service stand. To have the service stand clean and in best order is the first duty of *mise en place*. A good service stand should not have doors, as doors slow down the service. When the service stand has doors, a waiter wanting to pick up a glass or something else must bend down (which is extra work) to open the door, often finding there is no space to swing the door open. It is not surprising to see a busy waiter closing the door with his foot.

A well-arranged service stand should contain everything a waiter might possibly need during the service rush. Every trip to the kitchen or to the dishwasher for a spoon or glass is only wasted energy and time.

The following indispensible items should be stored in a well arranged service stand: 1) table-cloth; 2) napkins; 3) plates; 4) glasses; 5) silver; 6) ashtrays; 7) salt and pepper shakers; 8) different spices and sauces; and 9) a *rechaud*.* All should be within easy reach so that the waiter can speed up his service and reset tables quickly.

Mise en place includes not only the cleaning and refilling of the service stand, but also the cleaning and refilling of salt and pepper shakers, spice bottles, the setting of tables, dusting of chairs, and arranging of flowers. This is all done prior to the opening of the dining room.

The Service

French service differs from other services in that all food is served from a *gueridon* (cart). The *gueridon*, covered with a tablecloth, is kept close to the guest's table. It must have a *rechaud* to keep food warm. The *gueridon* should be the same height as the guest's table.

In French service, the food is partially prepared by the chef in the kitchen, and is "finished" by the *chef de rang* in view of the guests. Food is brought into the dining room on an attractive silver platter by the *commis de rang* who sets it on the *rechaud* to keep warm. The *chef de rang* then takes over. First, he presents the platter to the guests to admire and approve, and next he carves the meat or bones the fish or chicken and makes the sauce or any garnishes required.

The *commis de rang* holds each guest's plate below the silver platter while the *chef de rang*, using both hands, transfers the food, which the guest selects, from the silver platter to the guest's plate. The *chef de rang* may hold the serving fork and spoon in one hand, to leave the other hand free. *(See illustration, top of page 13.)* This practice is acceptable when no *commis* is near to help him, so that he must hold the plate himself while serving the food.

Once the food has been arranged on the plate, the *commis de rang* takes the plate in his *right* hand and serves it to the guest from the guest's *right* side. *(See illustration on page 14.)*

---
* A small heater with a candle or sterno used to keep food warm.

In French service, everything is served from the right with the exception of the butter and the bread plates, salad plates, and any other extra dish which should be placed at the left side of the guest. Every rule has its reason. To serve food from the right is much easier for a right-handed waiter as he can carry the plate in his right hand, and set the tray in front of a guest from the right. It is difficult and awkward to serve a plate with your right hand from the left side. The exception to the rule is when a waiter is left-handed: then he may serve from the left instead of the right.

Soup

When guests order soup, it is brought into the dining room in a silver bowl and placed on the *rechaud* to keep warm. More soup than needed is always brought in. Soup not ladled out into the guest's soup plate is brought back to the chef and reheated to serve other guests.

The *commis* also brings hot soup plates. The soup plate is then placed on an *hors d'oeuvre* plate with a square folded napkin in between the *hors d'oeuvre* plate and the soup plate. This napkin serves a dual purpose: 1) it makes it possible for the waiter to carry the plate without getting burned; and 2) it prevents the waiter from putting his thumb into the soup. This service is more attractive than placing only the regular soup plate before the guest. The soup is ladled from the silver bowl into the soup plate by the *chef de rang* and served to the guest by the *commis* — or the waiter — from the right with the *right* hand.

Main Course

The main course, or any other course in French service, is served in the same manner as the soup course. The *chef de rang* always does the carving, preparing, or flaming of a course, and arranges it on the guest's plate; the *commis* serves it. When a chateaubriand steak for two persons is to be served, the cooked filet with the *grand jus*, potatoes and vegetables, come from the kitchen. Then the *chef de rang* prepares the sauce in front of the guest, reheats the chateaubriand, carves, and arranges the food on the guest's plate, meanwhile watching the guest to see what size portion he desires. Salad is served with the main course and placed below the butter plate with the *left* hand from the *left* side of the guest.

The Correct Way to Hold Plates

Plates should be held with the thumb, index finger, and the middle finger. The upper part of the plate's rim should not be touched; this prevents fingers from getting into the soup or leaving marks on the plate. The technique is not so difficult as it sounds — have someone demonstrate it and then try it. *(See Illustration 7, page 11.)*

Clearing the Table

Clear the table after all guests have finished eating. To clear the table while one or two guests are still eating is rude and ill mannered, making these slow diners feel rushed. A restaurant using French service does not look for high turnover. Give the guests a chance to dine leisurely and to enjoy the service and the meal. Before serving the dessert, make sure that the table is brushed and that clean ashtrays are brought in.

Removing the Plates

Over-specialization in food service with little regard for the problems of the dish room are often, and perhaps justly, criticized. Formerly, "The Three S's" — *scrape, stack,* and *separate* were standard procedures. Partial scraping, stacking, and separation of china, glassware and silver by dining room personnel is labor-saving, results in neater trays and side stands, and, above all, cuts down on breakage and noise. *(See Illustration 9, page 11.)*

Never stack the plates in front of a guest. Always clear the table completely in one round. Going back and forth to the side stand with every plate is unprofessional and a waste of time. Training and experience will give the smoothness and precision in clearing a table that characterizes French service. Remove the salt and pepper after the main course is cleared — they are not needed with the dessert course.

Finger bowl

Finger bowls are served with all dishes that the guest eats with his fingers; such as, chicken, lobster, and fresh fruit. The finger bowl is a small silver or glass bowl placed on a silver underliner with a doily in between the bowl and the underliner. A clean, extra napkin is served with it. The finger bowl is filled only one-third full with warm water to prevent splashing. A lemon wedge or flower petals are often put into the water.

The finger bowl is served *with* the courses mentioned above, not afterwards. When a guest eating lobster with his fingers suddenly wishes a

Finger bowl ends French service.

sip of wine, he washes his fingers before touching the glass. If possible, place the finger bowl in front of the plate. An additional finger bowl is *always* served at the end of *any complete* meal in French service and is placed directly in front of the guest — with a fresh napkin. (*See illustration above.*)

Setups for Special Dishes:

Cold or hot Lobster and Langouste: Cold or hot dinner plate (depending on whether the lobster is served hot or cold), fish fork and fish knife, lobster fork, nut cracker, butter plate and butter knife, and finger bowl.

Caviar: Cold *hors d'oeuvre* plate, small *hors d'oeuvre* fork and knife, teaspoon, butter plate and butter knife.

Oysters and Clams: Oysters or clams are usually served arranged on crushed ice on silver platters. Many times this silver platter is placed in front of the guest with no extra plate. On other occasions the oysters are placed in the center of the table, the guest having an *hors d'oeuvre* plate on which to place his oysters. An oyster fork, butter plate, and butter knife, and a finger bowl are also included.

Whole Grilled Snails: Hot dinner plate, snail fork, snail tongs, butter plate and butter knife, and finger bowl are needed. The snails (fried in the shell and then arranged on a bed of heated salt on a silver platter) are placed in the center of the table. The snails are picked up with the snail tongs by the guest and are eaten with the special snail fork. This delicious light lunch is served with toast.

Fresh Fruits: Fruit or dessert plate, fruit fork and fruit knife, and finger bowl are necessary for

22

most fresh fruits. There are some exceptions; such as, mangos and papayas.

Fresh Grapes: Fresh grapes require a special service. The cover consists of a fruit or dessert plate, a crystal bowl or champagne saucer filled with ice water, a pair of scissors, fruit fork and fruit knife, and a finger bowl. The reason for this elaborate setup is that in French service the bunch of grapes is served in a crystal bowl in the center of the table. The guest then takes the pair of scissors, clips off a bunch of grapes, washes them in the ice water in the champagne saucer, and then puts the grapes on his plate. He eats the grapes with his fingers or uses the fruit fork and fruit knife to peel off the skin and take out the seeds.

Flaming

The restaurateur knows that flaming adds little taste to a dish but that it presents a gala and profitable display — so he encourages it. Flaming entrées and desserts impress the guest. The waiter, while flaming the dessert at one table, catches the attention of other people in the dining room who often order the same dessert. In flaming, the principle is always the same. The sauce or liqueur used is the only variation.

One of the world's most popular desserts is *Crêpes Suzette.* Like some other famous foods, *Crêpes Suzette* were first served quite by accident about a hundred years ago.

Henri Charpentier, chef to Edward, Prince of Wales, was making a complicated *crêpe* sauce. This sauce was a blend of orange and lemon peels, sugar, butter, Grand Marnier, Cointreau and Kirschwässer. By accident, the cordial caught fire and the young chef thought both he and his sauce were ruined. Since it was impossible to start again, Henri tasted the sauce and found it was delicious. He quickly put the *crêpes* into the liquid, added more cordials, and let the sauce burn again.

The Prince was delighted with the new dessert and named it after the lady with whom he was dining.

Steps in Preparing Crêpes Suzette:

1. Sprinkle granulated sugar in a hot pan, place over a low flame. Stir until sugar melts.
2. In a napkin, hold first the orange, and next the lemon in your hand, trim off the peels and put them into the pan. Stir with sugar.
3. Add butter. Stir mixture until the butter melts.

Crepes Suzette

Above: Sprinkle sugar in a chafing dish to prepare Crepes Suzette. *Right:* With a fork and spoon, roll heated Crepes Suzette in the sauce before flaming.

23

CREPE SUZETTE

Yield:	12 six-inch diameter Crêpes
Portion:	3 Crêpes per serving
Pan:	8-inch thin frying pan

Ingredients	Weights	Measures	Method
Flour, sifted all purpose		1 cup	1. Mix the dry ingredients together. Combine the liquid ingredients with the dry and beat until smooth—the batter should be the consistency of thin cream.
Sugar		1 Tbsp	2. Place a small amount of butter in the frying pan; heat until butter bubbles.
Salt		pinch	
Eggs, well beaten		1	3. Pour enough batter into the pan to spread to a six-inch circle. Rotate the pan quickly to spread the batter thinly and evenly.
Milk		1 cup	4. Cook Crêpe for about 1 minute; turn and cook on the other side.
Butter		2 Tbsp	5. With the aide of a fork and spoon, carefully roll the Crêpe.
			6. Repeat until all batter is used or 12 Crêpes have been baked.

CREPE SUZETTE SAUCE

Yield:	4 servings
Portion:	
Equipment:	Crêpe Suzette pan

Ingredients	Weights	Measures	Method
Sugar		½ cup	1. Caramelize ¼ cup of the sugar over low heat—stir sugar as it is caramelizing. Add the peelings of the orange and lemon.
Orange peel		½ orange	
Lemon peel		½ lemon	2. Add the butter to the caramelized sugar and stir until butter is melted.
Butter		¼ cup	3. Add the juice of the orange and lemon. Cook a few minutes—remove the peelings.
Orange juice		½ orange	
Lemon juice		½ lemon	4. Place the Crêpes into the sauce.
Cognac	1 oz.	2 Tbsp	5. Sprinkle the remaining ¼ cup sugar over the Crêpes. Add half of the Cognac, Grand Marnier and Cointreau. Carefully reroll the Crêpes, add the remaining Cognac, Grand Marnier and Cointreau.
Grand Marnier	1 oz.	2 Tbsp	
Cointreau	1 oz.	2 Tbsp	6. Tip the pan so the flame touches the liquor and ignites sauce. Serve Crêpes (3 to a serving), using fork and spoon, on hot dessert plates.

Variation: 1) Grated orange & lemon rind may be used and left in the sauce or large pieces of orange & lemon may be placed in the sugar 24 hours before the sugar is to be caramelized. The sugar absorbs the flavor of the orange & lemon. Then remove.

2) Pre-prepared, orange-flavored butter can be used to save time and labor. To prepare, mix finely grated orange and lemon peel with the sugar and combine with whipped butter for use in step 1.

4. Squeeze orange and lemon juice into the pan; remove orange and lemon peels.

5. Put *crêpes* into pan — unroll, warm, and turn them.

6. Roll *crêpes* — and let them simmer in juice.

7. Add some more granulated sugar on top of *crêpes*.

8. Add Grand Marnier, Cointreau, and Cognac (brandy).

9. Dip the pan so the flame below touches the Cognac and ignites the whole sauce.

10. Serve *crêpes*, using fork and spoon, on hot dessert plates.

As mentioned before, French service, despite its grandeur, has both advantages and disadvantages:

Advantages:
- French service gives the guest the greatest possible personal attention.
- It makes the guest feel very important — royal treatment. It is showy.

Disadvantages:
- It is more expensive and needs a larger professional staff.
- To use *gueridons,* French service requires more dining room space and reduces the number of seats in the dining room.
- French service is a slow service.

Line of Authority in Dining Room

In American Service:	In French Service:
Food and Beverage Manager	*Maitre d'Hotel*
Director of Service	*Chef de Service*
Wine Steward	*Chef de Vin*
Head Waiter	*Chef de Salle*
Captain	*Chef d'Etage*
Waiter	*Chef de rang*
Bus Boy	{ *Demi-Chef de Rang* *Commis de rang* *Apprentice*

Explanation of Kitchen Names

Grosse Brigade	A large kitchen crew.
Chef de Cuisine	The chef of the kitchen.
Sous - Chef	Second chef, the chef's right-hand man.
Saucier	Sauce cook, in charge of sauces, gravies and stews.
Rotisseur	Roast cook
Restaurateur	Cook in charge of all "a la carte" orders.
Garde Manger	Cold meat man.
Entremétier	Cook in charge of garniture, vegetables, etc.
Légumier	Vegetable cook.
Potager	Soup cook.
Poissonnier	Fish cook.
Patissier	Pastry cook.
Tournant	Relief cook; must know all parts of the kitchen.

The Classical Menu Skeleton

In French:	In English:
Hors d'oeuvre froid	Cold *hors d'oeuvre*
Hors d'oeuvre chaud	Hot *hors d'oeuvre*
Potages	Soups
Poissons	Fish
Grosse-Pièce	Main dish
Entrées chauds	Hot extra dishes
Entrées froids	Cold extra dishes
Rotis, Salades	Roasts and Salads
Légumes	Vegetables
Entréments, Desserts	Pastries and Desserts
Fromage	Cheese
Fruit	Fruit

Line of Authority in French Kitchen

In addition to the various stations shown in the chart below, there is an announcer or *abboyeur* (generally the *chef de cuisine*) who takes the orders from waiters and passes them to the various cooks. This prevents arguments between the waiters and cooks and also speeds up the issuing of food.

A Grosse Brigade

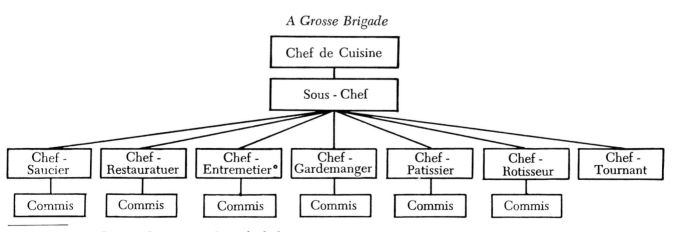

° *Legumier, Potager, Poissonnier* — Instead of *chef entremetier* in larger kitchens.

5. Russian Service

Today Russian service (in America often erroneously called "French service"), is the most popular dining room service in all of the better restaurants and hotels in the world. As the name implies, Russian service originated in Russia, making its first appearance on the European continent during the Napoleonic wars. At that time, the old-fashioned English service and the cumbersome French service were still the dominant types used in Europe.

In English service, food comes in whole pieces from the kitchen, is presented to the guests, and then is either cut by the host or removed and cut elsewhere.

French service also has its disadvantages. True, most dishes come precut from the kitchen, but service is made from a *gueridon*, placed adjacent to every diner's table. Not only is this service slow, but it also requires a great deal of space.

Russian service, because of its simplicity and speed, soon proved its advantages. It became the most popular and fashionable method of serving in every royal court and is now used in luxury-type restaurants. Today, English service has disappeared on the European continent, and French service can only be found in a few, old-fashioned, high-class restaurants.

The table arrangement, in Russian service, is identical to the arrangement for French service, but the service itself differs. In Russian service, the food is fully prepared and precut in the kitchen and is then neatly arranged on silver platters by the chef. These platters are brought into the dining room by the waiter, who serves the guest from these platters.

The waiter orders the food in the kitchen the same as in American service; but when the waiter comes back to pick up the food, he receives it on silver platters rather than on serving plates. He carries the hot plates and the silver platter with the food on one large tray into the dining room. He first sets the tray with the food and the empty plates on a side stand. Then he picks up the plates and sets them before the guest from the guest's *right,* using the *right* hand. (Again the old rule: plates are set in from the *right.*) By doing so, the waiter goes around the table *clockwise,* which enables him to go forward instead of backward.

After the plates are placed, the waiter returns to his side stand, picks up and holds the silver

In Russian service, food is transferred from a silver platter onto the plate before the guest. Cover is the same as for French service.

platter on his left hand and serves the guest from the left with his right hand. *(See illustration above.)*

The reason for serving from the left is that the waiter must hold the silver platter on his left hand in order to use his right hand for serving the food with fork and spoon. If he were to try serving from the right, the waiter would cross his hands and most likely dip his sleeve in the gravy. Therefore, the golden rule for Russian service is: *Set empty plates in from the right by going around the table clockwise. Serve the food from the silver platter from the left by going around the table counterclockwise.*

Before food is served, it is a nice gesture to present the silver platter to the host or to the party. This gives the guests an opportunity to see what the chef has arranged on the platter and most likely the beautiful arrangement of food stimulates the appetite. *(See illustrations, page 7.)*

When serving the food, the waiter has some leeway regarding the amount he serves. He can please the guest by giving him the portion he wants. Any food not served from the silver platter always goes directly back to the chef in the kitchen.

In brief, the principal technique of Russian service is that every food item is brought into the dining room, not on a plate as in American service, but on a silver platter from which it is then served by the waiter to the guest's plate, which has been previously placed before the guest.

This rule holds for soup service except when soup is served in a cup. If the soup is served in a soup plate, the hot soup plate is put on an *hors d'oeuvre* plate with a square-folded napkin between the two plates (as in French service) and placed empty in front of the guest. Then the soup is brought to the guest either in a large silver bowl from which it is ladled into the soup plate, or in a silver cup from which it is poured into the soup plate. This is the only occasion in Russian service where two methods may be used.

Since all work can be done alone by one waiter, Russian service has a great advantage over French service, for which two waiters are needed.

Because its popularity is increasing in most first-class hotels and restaurants, one can assume that Russian service has many advantages in comparison to other types of services. The advantages of Russian service are:

- Only one waiter is needed per station.
- It is a fast service.
- It is less expensive than most other services.
- It is an elegant and high-class service.
- No extra space is needed for equipment.
- It guarantees equal portions because they are pre-cut in the kitchen.
- There is less waste because food not served is returned to the chef to be reused instead of being discarded into the garbage can.
- It gives the guest personal attention.

But, like other things in life, Russian service is not perfect and has disadvantages:

- There is a big initial investment in silver equipment.
- If many guests are to be served from one silver platter, the last guest served may see a rather unappetizing serving platter.
- If every guest in a party orders a different dish (like steak and fish) the waiter must carry too many different silver platters from the kitchen to the dining room.

"Service is the cheerful giving of attention" framed over the ingoing door reminds each waiter that cheerfulness does more to insure the guest's pleasant meal than does the most expert service. *"If you're not proud of it, don't serve it,"* over the left door is management's carte blanche to the waiter to check the product. The waiter, given this authority, should be backed up by the management.

(*Right*) Banquet glasses can be filled with water quickly and efficiently by using a flexible hose attached to the refrigerated water system. Whole trays or racks of glasses with ice can be filled to a carefully gauged level through this apparatus.

6. Buffet Service

Buffets, smorgasbords, and "hunt breakfasts" are becoming increasingly popular styles of food service. Americans, accustomed to self-service, enjoy helping themselves to food attractively displayed. For seasonal and other festive occasions, buffet tables can be elaborately decorated and lighted. Moreover, fewer people may be needed in the kitchen during serving hours because cold food can be prepared in advance and the hot food is a set menu.

At the de luxe buffet, guests are served appetizers and soups at their tables before they go to the buffet. Beverages, bread and butter, and desserts are also usually served at the table by a waiter. The table set up for this reason is very much the same as that for regular table service. But, as the waiter can serve more people, his gratuities may be higher.

When no table service is provided, buffet space must be arranged for appetizers, table silver, bread and butter, desserts, and beverages. The typical arrangement is to set the guest plates at the beginning of the buffet table line and to place table silver, napkins, and bread and butter at the end. Separate islands for appetizers, for beverage service, and also for desserts speed buffet service and eliminate traffic congestion.

A supervisor should constantly be on duty to oversee the coordination of buffet service and kitchen preparation. It is desirable to have service personnel in crisp white chef uniforms stationed behind the buffet tables to:

1. Serve as hosts who offer, explain, and serve food.

2. Carve roasts and serve them.

3. Maintain the food display and the guest plate supply.

4. Check on equipment for keeping food hot or cold.

5. Administer "first aid" when a guest spills food or creates an unsightly spot.

Stage Managing Your Buffet

Select a special theme for your buffet and carry this idea through in backdrops, table decorations, and food merchandising. The theme can be seasonal—Christmas, Valentine, St. Patrick's Day, Easter, Mother's Day, July Fourth, etc. It can relate to community interests—local products, athletic events, music, art, or literary happenings, and so on. Or if the buffet is planned for a special group, use their insignia or product as your theme—paper products for a paper company, potato designs for the potato growers, automobiles for the car dealers, Rotary's "wheel" and company emblems.

Neatly dressed service attendants add human interest to buffet food service. Platters and trays of different shapes and sizes give variety to the food display.

Extra showmanship can be attained through the use of wall backdrops, decorated screens and trellises of laths or fence wire, potted palms, ferneries, flags, and mobile arrangements. Canopies of flameproofed striped awning or thatched palm can be built over a buffet island for desserts, fruits, or cold food. White linoleum rolls can be used to simulate huge candles, especially effective when combined with dark blue or dark red cloths for Easter or Christmas buffets. Burlap cloths give a rustic air to a buffet display, while red-and-white checked cloths provide informality.

Highlight your food display with spotlights and accent lights, so that light for dining can be kept to 5–10 foot candles. Introduce movement for flags and mobile hangings by directing a fan breeze on them from a wall location.

Arranging the Tables

Allow liberal table space for the food display so that people will be serving themselves at the buffet rather than standing in line. People average about one food selection per lineal foot. Thus, the number of items to be offered times the number of people to be served within a specified interval must be considered. Otherwise turnover will be slow and people will be waiting in line or at their tables.

Long tables can be arranged to form V-shapes, U-shapes, L-shapes, zig-zags, and hollow squares. When serpentines, half-rounds and quarter-rounds are available, it is possible to create ovals, S-shapes, and a variety of other arrangements. Tables can also be separated to form islands for certain entrees such as roasts, although a hazard is created when guests must carry full plates through a crowd. When desserts are not served at the guest

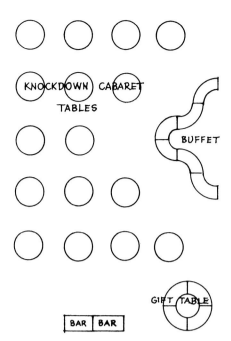

This schematic layout for buffet service shows a "gift table" island which could first be used for hors d'oeuvres and later on for a display of desserts.

tables, a special "dessert island" can be set up away from the main buffet and given extra decorative treatment: a Vienna or French pastry shop, an old-fashioned ice cream bar, a plantation melon patch, a Polynesian fruit panorama are just a few ideas.

Tablecloths should extend to about two inches from the floor; that is, they should be long enough to hide table supports but not long enough to be stepped on or catch heels in. Colored cloths and the use of pleating or frilling can provide interest to an otherwise long expanse of table cloth.

A "skyline" can be created for the buffet by building a second tier at the back of the display

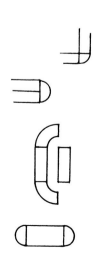

FOLDING TABLE SHAPES

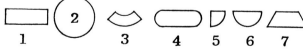

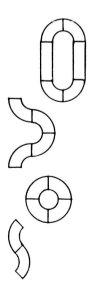

1. **Oblong**
2. **Round**
3. **Serpentine**
4. **Oval**
5. **Quarter-round**
6. **Half-round**
7. **Trapezoid**

Folding tables come with various shaped tops which are identified in the above diagrams. These shapes can be used to make many graceful buffet set-ups as shown in the combinations diagrammed in the margin. Serpentine shaped tables are particularly versatile.

Drawings courtesy of Institutional Products, Inc.

Seasonal buffet themes—Christmas, St. Valentine's, St. Patrick's, Easter, July Fourth—make the decorations easy to plan. In the buffet shown, the Yuletide theme is developed through a toy train to hold platters on the cold food table in the foreground. Red and green salad molds are displayed over light boxes which reflect red or green light up through the mold. Behind the hot food table is a toy-studded Santa's Workshop backdrop against which red and green lights are alternately played and a Christmas tree. On the hot food table, a series of silver trays holding vegetables are kept heated by electric units covered with silver foil, and an infra-red lamp keeps hot the Steamship Round of Beef. A buffet skyline is created on both tables by means of cloth-covered boxes. *Photograph courtesy of Smorgasbord Class, Cornell University.*

Each Food Display Should Have Eye Appeal.

Jewel-like salad molds can be mounted on covered boxes to give buffet tables a colorful skyline.

Chuck wagons, fish boats, and salad stalls can be made into colorful islands to merchandise buffet food and carry out special themes. Cheese tables and wine displays can receive similar treatment.

Buffet Themes Provide Decor Ideas

Every item on this attractively arranged cold meat tray is edible—as it should be.

Glazed peach tarts with cream peaks invite the buffet guest to select this dessert from a display of tortes and other cakes. *Photographs courtesy of Mr. John Dee.*

Ice sculpture gives glamour to a buffet. Many pieces are easy to do and can be reused. For instructions, see pages 66-68.

White linoleum rolls with votive candles inserted at the top make impressive candles. Color can be added with ribbon bows.

table. Height can also be introduced by placing some specialties, such as decorated hams, turkeys, and aspic molds, on pedestals. Epergnes, candelabra, floral and fruit arrangements, and ice carvings also add height and variety. Expanses that would otherwise be bare can be filled in with flat floral sprays of fern, smilax, holly or lemon leaves, and with cornucopias of fruit with flowers.

Food Display

Food should be placed on the table according to a pre-arranged plan which takes into consideration food relationships in the regular menu selection. The usual order is: 1) guest plates; 2) salads, relishes, molded dishes, smoked fish, cheeses, etc.; 3) hot vegetables; 4) roasts and other hot entrees. Sauces, dressings, and garnitures should be placed beside the dish they accompany—mayonnaise with the salad, cranberry sauce with the turkey and so on. Large divided "wheels" on turntables can be used for relish displays or for fresh fruits such as whole strawberries and assortments of melon balls. When such a "wheel" is not available, a large tray with sections of folded foil will serve the same purpose.

When there is sufficient variety of cold items and hot vegetables, the number of hot entrees can be limited, an important point in keeping down food cost and the number of kitchen workers needed on duty. Low-cost hot entrees, such as Swedish Meatballs and Chicken Cacciatore, can be attractively displayed so that guests fill their plates with these items instead of more costly roasts. Sometimes the buffet is presented in two phases: the guest goes first to the cold buffet and then makes a second trip for hot food. A full plate of salads, gelatin molds, and appetizers will reduce the amount of food the guest chooses for his hot plate.

Low-cost hot entrees might also include such international cook-yourself tidbits as *Boeuf Bourguignonne*, Cheese Rarebits, Shish Kebabs, and Thailand's chicken or seafood cooked in a Mongolian hot pot. These should be set up on separate islands as conversational cooking centers and presided over by serving personnel garbed in the costume of the nation whose food is being featured. The server's role is to see that the food to be cooked is pre-prepared, explain the food, and tell guests how to cook it. In somewhat similar fashion curries can be displayed already prepared in chafing dishes with all of the accompanying condiments and garnishes.

In arranging the food display, consideration must be given to chafing dishes and electric heating plates to keep food hot and bowls of shaved ice to keep food cold. Attendants should keep an eye on chafing dishes to make sure the flame is operating properly. Bowls of ice may need frequent replacement. Lighted candles must be kept straight and free of dripping wax. To avoid guest accidents, chafing dishes and candles should be set well back from the serving line. In all instances, it is wise to place food platters and trays two to three inches back of the table's edge.

Silver chafing dishes with sterno lamps give a buffet elegance.

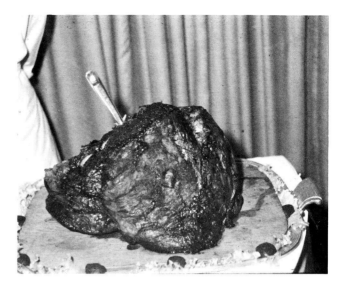

People seldom see such a huge roast as this Steamship Round of Beef. Thus it makes a spectacular showpiece when carved before guests.

Maintaining the Display

Service personnel, in addition to being attentive to guests, should see that a serving dish is replaced with a full one before the first is one-third empty. A nearly empty dish is unsightly and detracts from the bountiful-food idea so important in buffet merchandising of low-cost items. When a replacement is needed, a word to the buffet supervisor will enable him to alert kitchen runners to bring one in.

An adequate supply of hot and cold guest plates should always be available. Extra serving utensils should be readily at hand for the staff behind the tables and also clean napkins and damp cloths for tidying displays and spills.

Carving Roasts

Buffet service typically features a huge roast of the type seldom cooked at home, which is carved by a chef at the buffet. The chef, although he carves while guests look on, should have a few slices of meat readily available on a heated platter to keep the serving line moving.

Popular roasts include Standing Rib Roast of Beef, "Steamship" Round*, Ham and Turkey. (Diagrams for carving these roasts are given on

_____
* The "Steamship" Round is the wholesale straight-cut (or V-cut) beef round from which the vertebrae, aitch-bone and shank have been removed before roasting. The lower end of the femur bone is left in the roast and the rump is tied to the top round to produce a neat compact roast of 50 to 60 pounds.

the next pages.) The carver should have a knife with a good blade which he keeps properly steeled before and during his carving. Buffet portions are sliced thin and are about one-half or one-third the portions presented in regular table service. The idea is that the guest may wish to help himself to other meat entrees or return for a second helping.

In carving roast beef, keep the cutting board neat and tidy by wiping up blood and scraping off hardened fat. Arrange parsley sprigs or curly endive around the board's perimeter to make it look attractive. Natural gravy (au jus) should be kept warm in a silver boat over a candle heater, from which the server may help the guests. When guests prefer their beef well done and no well done sections are available, spoon a little hot juice over a few cut slices to quickly "cook" them.

Guest Accidents

When a guest spills food on the table, the serving personnel should quickly and inobtrusively brush the food onto a plate, lightly clean the spot with a damp cloth and then cover it with a clean napkin. If a guest spills food on the carpet in front of the table, call this to the attention of the buffet supervisor who will have a busboy immediately remove the spillage. A white napkin quickly laid over the spilled food will alert other guests not to step on it and grind it into the carpet. If a guest spills food on his or another's clothing, direct the supervisor's attention to this mishap and he will see that an attendant offers first aid away from the scene.

7. Banquet Service

Banquet service needs separate treatment, although the basic techniques are similar to those presented in previous chapters. The American, French, and Russian types of service, previously discussed, have all had these disadvantages:

- How many guests will come is not known.
- What dishes the guests will order is not known with any certainty.
- No definite hour is set when the guests will arrive.

In banquet service, the reverse is true: the management knows exactly when the guests are coming, how many of them there will be, and what they are going to eat. This is of great help to the management, to the kitchen staff, and to the banquet staff.

When a banquet is booked, one copy of the order goes to the chef and one to the banquet maitre d'hotel. The order includes the number of persons expected, the time the banquet begins, and the complete dinner menu. With this information, the banquet staff's job is greatly simplified. The tables must be set at a specific time and for a specific number of guests. The individual covers are set with the plates, silverware, and glassware needed for the particular meal.

Two types of service are commonly used in banquet service, the merits of which will be discussed later in this chapter.

Setting a Banquet Table

The *mise en place* or preparation for a banquet is similar to the preparations made in the main dining room. No major difference is made in setting up individual covers, but everything needed by the guest during the dinner is placed on the table, when it is being set, in the exact order to be used by the guest.

The first step in setting a banquet table, as in setting any other table, is fastening the silence cloth (*molton*), which is necessary when no permanent silence cloth is attached to the table. On top of the silence cloth, place the tablecloth. (*See Illustration 10, page 10.*) The tablecloth can be spread by one person on a small table; but if the table is large it should be spread by two or four persons to avoid wrinkles. If several tablecloths are used on a long table, the center creases must meet to give a continuous line from one end of the table to the other. The tablecloth should extend at least 12" over each edge of the table (to the edge of the chair) but should not be long enough to interfere with the comfort of the guests. (*See Illustration 11, page 10.*)

After the tablecloth is properly laid, place the napkins, silverware, glassware, and plates in position. Time can be saved by using assembly line techniques. Time is wasted when each waiter sets his own station; organized and combined efforts

BANQUET AND BUFFET TABLE ARRANGEMENTS

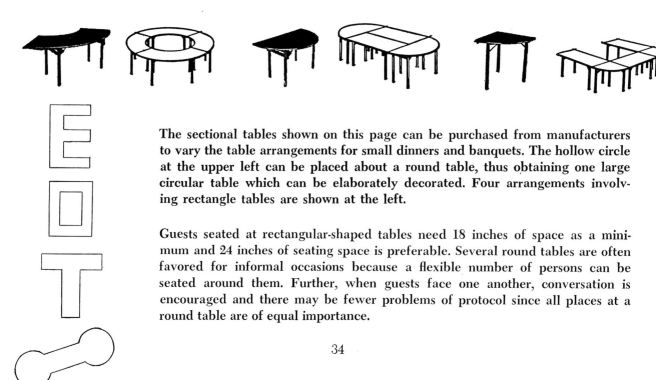

The sectional tables shown on this page can be purchased from manufacturers to vary the table arrangements for small dinners and banquets. The hollow circle at the upper left can be placed about a round table, thus obtaining one large circular table which can be elaborately decorated. Four arrangements involving rectangle tables are shown at the left.

Guests seated at rectangular-shaped tables need 18 inches of space as a minimum and 24 inches of seating space is preferable. Several round tables are often favored for informal occasions because a flexible number of persons can be seated around them. Further, when guests face one another, conversation is encouraged and there may be fewer problems of protocol since all places at a round table are of equal importance.

This formal dinner table is shown as it will greet the guests. The fresh fruit appetizer in half a pineapple rests on a glass underliner over the china service plate. The outer teaspoon points to the glass in which white win will be served, the steak knife to the glass for red wine. Napkins, folded crown-style (see page 62) are set on the bread and butter plate. If a fish fork is used instead of an extra dinner fork, it could be laid parallel to the service plate, crossed with the demitasse spoon.

require much less time. Depending upon the menu ordered or the policy of the house, the first thing to be set on the table will be the *hors d'oeuvre* plate. One waiter rolls a cart in from the kitchen with all of the hors d'oeuvre plates required for the banquet. Then, taking a stack of plates in his left hand, he proceeds around the tables clockwise, setting one plate for each cover. The *hors d'oeuvre* plate is the starting point for the other items that go on the table.

The second waiter follows the first waiter with the napkins. A third waiter follows the second waiter, carrying dinner knives in a napkin in his left hand, and places them (using his right hand) to the right of the plate with the blade of the knife facing towards the plate. A fourth waiter,

in the same manner, places the forks to the left of the plate. Other waiters follow with additional items needed for the table. Silverware is never carried in the hand. Hold all silverware in a napkin or carry it on a plate to prevent fingermarks on the silver. (See illustrations on pages 10–11.)

In high-class banquet service, each guest has a set of salt and pepper shakers and an ashtray. If space is limited (as at a table for ten) set three at each table. Four or five persons should never be expected to share one big ashtray. Flower arrangements are put on the table last. Low arrangements are preferable, so that the guests need not peek around or through the flowers to converse with the person across the table. (See illustration below.)

This informal banquet table, set for ten, shows the seafood forks for the appetizer laid with the tines inside the teaspoon. Flower arrangement is kept low so that guests can see one another. Only three ashtrays, three salt and pepper sets, and two sugar bowls are used to conserve space.

American Banquet Service

The covers for American service at banquets differ from those used for Russian service. In American banquet service, if no *hors d'oeuvre* plate is required for the first course, the napkin is placed at the cover for each guest.

- Place the dinner knife to the right of the napkin with the edge towards the napkin; next to the knife, place the soup spoon; and then the two coffee spoons.*
- To the left of the napkin, place a dinner fork and then a salad fork.
- The water goblet is placed at the tip of the knife.
- The butter plate holding a butter knife is placed at the tip of the forks.

  (The butter knife may either be placed across the top of the butter plate, parallel to the edge of the table, or placed across the right side of the butter plate, parallel to the other silverware with the cutting edge to the left.)

- The coffee cup is sometimes placed on the table before the guests come in and the cup and saucer are placed above the knife. (Although it is not very elegant and not recommended, placing the coffee cup on the table before the guests come in saves time and is often done for less expensive parties.)
- Sugars and creamers are placed between each two covers and above the knives and forks.

In American banquet service, the water goblets should be filled with ice water before the guests sit down. Butter and bread or rolls are placed on the butter plates. The food is served on plates in the kitchen, the waiter carrying the plates to the dining room, and setting a plate before each guest from the guest's *left* with his *left* hand. All dishes are served and removed from the *left* with the *left* hand except beverages, which are served from the guest's right.

The advantage of using American banquet service is that less skill is required.

- Waiters carry in trays holding plates of food topped with covers.
- Food, to be served hot, must be placed on the plates shortly before it is served, or kept hot in holding cabinets.
- Every plate must be handled and garnished separately by production line or production "square" methods.

---

* Even though silver is not placed in the order which the food is eaten, the American public is accustomed to this setting and many insist the arrangement looks better.

Russian Banquet Service

Russian banquet service is more complicated and requires professional waiters. Generally it is used for expensive banquets.

The following could be the menu served:

Canapes Royal
(Little canapes with salmon, gooseliver, caviar.)

Consomme Double au Sherry
(Strong consomme with sherry)

Truite au Bleu
Pommes Persille
(Blue boiled trout with parsleyed potatoes)

Tournedos a la Rossini
Haricots Verts
Pommes Parisienne
(A filet mignon with gooseliver, truffles, and Madeira sauce. Green beans and small, round potatoes.)

Parfait d'Amour
(A decorated mold of rich ice cream with coffee flavor dominating.)

Cafe — Cognac — Liqueur

For this menu, start with an *hors d'oeuvre* plate. To its right, in order from the plate outward, place; 1) a dinner knife (or perhaps a steak knife); 2) a fish knife; 3) a soup spoon; and 4) an *hors d'oeuvre* knife. To the left from the plate, place: 1) a dinner fork; 2) a fish fork (somewhat higher than the dinner fork in order to save space); and 3), the *hors d'oeuvre* fork. These are placed in the order of the menu, with the last piece of silverware to be used placed next to the plate.

The dessert fork and spoon are placed above the plate, just as in the standard set-up for Russian or French service. (*See illustration on page 14.*) The butter plate is placed to the left of the hors d'oeuvre fork with the butter knife laid on it.

The wine glasses (Assume that two wines are ordered: a white wine and a red wine.) are set so that the glass for the first wine to be served is nearest to the guest's right. Thus, the red wine glass is placed at the tip of the dinner knife, and the white wine glass, slightly lower and closer to the guest's right. (*See illustration on page 45.*)

No sugar, creamer, or coffee cups are placed on the table. The coffee service is on a side stand ready to be served after the main course has been removed and the dessert has been served.

In Russian type banquet service, the food is brought into the dining room on silver platters with six, eight, or ten portions on one platter. A

A simple banquet menu can be made elaborate when the dessert is served with ceremony. Here chefs present Bombe Grand Marnier to persons at head table (of a banquet for 400) in a lotus blossom conveyance. Immediately afterward, waiters marched in with a dessert on a decorated platter for each table, where it was cut before the guests and served by the waiter. Conveyance can be used again and again.

hot plate is placed in front of each guest. Then, the food is served from the silver platter onto the plate of the guest from the guest's *left*, with the waiter's *left* hand as in regular Russian service. The correct wine is poured shortly before each course is served.

Russian service is without question the most exclusive and best-suited banquet service. Some advantages are:

- Elegance of service and "showmanship" when all the waiters come into the dining room simultaneously with their lavishly decorated silver platters.
- It speeds service and simplifies preparation in the kitchen.

- The chef has less work in preparing eight to ten silver platters than he would have when he must arrange a separate plate for each guest.
- The platter service takes less space, and it is easier to prepare the silver platters with food beforehand and keep the food warm than it is to keep several hundred plates warm.
- It is easier for a waiter to carry one silver platter than to carry ten plates.

In all types of banquet service, the serving must be done by all waiters simultaneously. The headwaiter, or whoever is in charge of the banquet, gives a signal. Then all waiters start serving or start clearing their stations. In larger establishments these signals may be given by signal light.

Cherries Jubilee, completed in the banquet room under lowered lights while tables are being cleared, provides a festive attraction for the guests. Ice cream balls, prepared in advance and held in the freezer, are dished in the kitchen into glass sherbet bowls. The large silver chafing dish holds pitted Bing cherries, preheated with juice-sauce in the kitchen. Orange and lemon rind and juice are added. The small chafing bowl contains heated Kirsch and brandy, which are flamed with showmanship before being poured into the cherry mixture. This in turn is spooned on the ice cream. About fifty guests can be served from one dessert cart.

This Statler Inn banquet table centerpiece groups champagne splits around a glass-enclosed candle with wreathes of greenery and fresh flowers. The bottles, whose neckbands give the event's name and date and labels present the menu, are guest souvenirs. The tulip glasses are filled with iced champagne, opened at the table.

Photograph courtesy of Great Western

Below

A Christmas village enchants old and young alike during the holidays at Cornell's Statler Inn. The structures and figurines were formed of Royal Frosting, with which they were also fastened and decorated. The skating pond is a mirror surrounded with icing snow. A similar effect can be achieved through trimming and decorating cookies and using candy and paper decorations for the figures.

JOHANNISBERG
RIESLING

FOLLE BLANCHE

CABERNET
SAUVIGNON

ZINFANDEL

GRENACHE

CHENIN BLANC

GAMAY
BEAUJOLAIS

PINOT
CHARDONNAY

GEWURTZTRAMINER

PINOT NOIR

SAUVIGNON
BLANC

Most of the great wines of the world are derived from the varieties of grapes pictured above. The exceptions are some New York State wines, which come from varietal grapes, and those produced in other regions largely for local consumption.

Reproduced with the permission of Almaden Vineyards. The wine obtained from the grapes pictured is influenced by the climate and soil of the vineyard in which they are grown. Yearly variations in sun, temperature, and rainfall affect the wine's quality in even the most ideal locations.

Principal Varieties of the World's Famous Wine Grapes

Wine and Beverage Service

JULIUS WILE
Senior Vice President
Julius Wile Sons and Co., Inc.

Wine and Bar Service

Julius Wile, Senior Vice President
Julius Wile Sons & Co., Inc.

Wine is important to good food service. First, wine adds to the profits of a hotel or restaurant. Second, the sale of a glass or bottle of wine adds to the guest's check, thereby automatically increasing the waiter's gratuity. Third, and perhaps even more important, good wine enjoyed with good food adds to the establishment's reputation. People will return often and recommend the place to their friends, thus causing the management and staff to prosper.

Moderate selling prices for wines are important. One of the problems of the hospitality field is that wines and spirits are put in the same category. Accountants generally state that the beverage department should show a profit higher than that made on food service. This is an erroneous assumption. The fallacy of this thinking is that once the diner has finished drinking aperitifs or cocktails and has ordered his meal, he will no longer have another cocktail — he is ready for something else.

That something else should be wine. Yet if wine is priced out of reach, the diner will not order it. Therefore, the establishment loses not only the drink he would not have bought anyway, but also loses the sale of wine. It has been proved by many restaurants and hotels that, when a moderate profit was taken on their wines, there was a marked increase in the sale of wine. It is astonishing how much wine can be sold just by calling it to people's attention with displays, mention of wine on the menu and by presenting the wine list as soon as the food is ordered.

Wine lists. The lists need not be complicated nor need they be very long. The list should be in line, however, with the type of restaurant in which it is being used. A good selection of five or ten wines is better than a poor selection of fifty. Wine lists should be simple. They should be up to date. And above all, they should be available and used. A menu which has changes and deletions is not acceptable in a good restaurant. Therefore it also follows that a wine list is not acceptable if it has changes or if items are out of stock.

The wine list should be as clear and clean and presentable as the menu from which the diner selects his food. Enough information should be given on the list so that the customer knows what he is ordering without having to ask questions. The type of wine, the size of the bottle, the name of the wine, its vintage if there is any, and the name of the shipper are all important information. Identifying each wine by a number is helpful since this practice eliminates embarrassment in pronunciation.

Vintages and wine charts. Because our climatic conditions are relatively stable year in and year out, the vintage on American wines means nothing other than an indication of the age of the wine. In Europe, vintages mean much more since certain years produce great wines, some mediocre wines and others poor wines. However, it is always true that a few poor wines are made in good years and a few good wines are made in relatively poor years.

Price is influenced by the size of the vintage, as a good year may produce a bumper crop which would mean that the prices would not be very high. Conversely, fine wines produced in a year when the quantity is low would tend to raise the prices out of proportion. Vintage charts are put out by the dozen. You will find that no two of them are alike. Therefore, remember that some good wines are produced in poor years, and some poor wines are produced in good years.

Wine sales. In Europe, both wine and food are ordered. In our country, food is ordered but wine must generally be sold. Where there is a *sommelier* or wine steward, this is his job.

When the waiter is responsible for the wine, he should present the wine list to the host immediately after the food has been ordered. It is good practice to leave the wine list so that it can be read. Then return in five minutes and ask which wine is desired.

The waiter will often be asked for advice. When recommending wine, let the customer lead you if possible. He may have a preference and there is no rule in the world that says he should not have a white wine with meat or red wine with fish if he so desires. Too often wine is *not* consumed because people are afraid of making a mistake. If

(*Above*)

In the Waldorf-Astoria's wine room, bottles of wine are stored in a horizontal position to keep the corks moist, thus excluding air. Each wine bin is numbered to correspond with the numbers on the hotel's wine list.

(*Right*)

The service refrigerator in the Bull & Bear restaurant of the Waldorf-Astoria holds white, rose, and sparkling wines chilled for immediate service in a wine cooler when ordered by a guest.

The unopened wine bottle, brought from the refrigerator, is presented to the host for his approval before it is placed in the wine cooler.

two people are dining together and one has meat and the other fish, let them choose what to have, or recommend a *vin rosé* which goes beautifully with either.

In the middle of the day when people plan returning to work, or don't wish a heavy meal, a white wine or *vin rosé* would be preferable, no matter what they are eating. Don't forget that wine comes in half-bottles and much wine can be sold by the glass. In summer time, wine and soda (sometimes called a "spritzer") served as a highball is a delightful thirst quencher.

Once the wine order is taken, the wine and glassware should be obtained promptly. This will enable service of the wine with the first course. Always ask first if the wine should be served in this manner. Sometimes the diners will request that wine be served with the main course; but often they will be happy to start with it at the beginning of the meal. As a result of this prompt service, the wine is consumed quicker and a second bottle of wine is frequently ordered.

Wine storage. If the wine cellar is remote, a small selection of the most popular wines should be kept in or close to the dining area. White, rosé and sparkling wines should be kept under refrigeration, so that they will be pre-chilled and available for prompt service and consumption. Red wines should also be available but kept at room temperature. Table wines should always be stored in horizontal position, as shown on the previous page. In this position, the wine remains in contact with the cork, keeping it moist and firm. Otherwise the cork would shrink, thus permitting air to enter the bottle and spoil the wine.

White and Rosé (Pink) Wines

White and rosé wines are served chilled. Traditionally, they are served with white meats—fowl, fish, and seafood. Turkey may be served with either white or red wine. Tradition does not rule out the possibility that white wine may be drunk with red meat. When a guest orders a particular type and brand of wine, he should be served the wine he orders with no comment by the waiter.

Presenting the wine. When a guest asks for white wine, the waiter—or *sommelier* (wine steward)—should obtain the bottle from storage, set it into an ice bucket, cover it with a clean, folded napkin and bring this service into the dining room. The ice bucket, placed on a stand, is set to the right of the person who ordered the wine. The waiter (or *sommelier*) then takes the bottle out of the bucket and presents it to the guest with the label uppermost. The host thus has an opportunity to verify the correctness of his order.

This bottle presentation is an important part of wine service and should not be overlooked. If the waiter misunderstood the guest and brought in the wrong wine—to which the guest will later object—the waiter can now readily exchange this bottle for one the guest prefers. Had the waiter ignored this presentation ritual and opened the bottle without showing it to the guest for his approval, the bottle would have to be returned to storage and may become a loss. Furthermore, this bottle-presentation ceremony shows courtesy to the guest, regardless of his knowledge about wines, and adds to the atmosphere of the dining room.

Wine glasses. Set the correct glasses on the table before opening the wine. For white wines, several types of stem glasses can be used. Some establishments prefer an "all-purpose" wine glass. Others use ornate, long-stemmed glassware that may be both expensive and fragile but which adds to the general atmosphere. For elaborate service the glasses in which white wine is to be served should have been previously chilled. When chilled glasses are not available, the waiter may chill them in crushed ice. Or the glasses may be filled with crushed ice while the wine is being inspected and opened. The ice should then be dumped into the ice bucket just prior to pouring the wine.

Opening the wine. The opening of the wine bottle begins with the removal of the foil around the cork and neck of the bottle. The foil should be cut with a knife well below the lip of the bottle and not ripped off with a fingernail. Older wines are often a bit moldy below the foil at the top of the cork. Wipe the bottle top and cork with a clean napkin. Set the corkscrew into the cork and turn it carefully straight down all the way, using only moderate pressure. Since a cork breaks easily, it is important that the corkscrew turns in straight, rather at an angle, to avoid broken cork bits falling into the bottle.

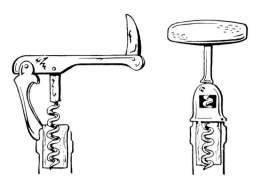

Corkscrews with levers and knife blades are liked by waiters, and "T" type automatic pullers by most waitresses. The cork should be penetrated fully before the pull is begun.

Pouring the wine. Before pouring any wine, wipe the open top of the bottle with a clean napkin to remove any cork grains or other impurities. The waiter should pour about an ounce into the glass of the host (or whoever ordered the wine) so that he can approve the wine. Hold a towel in the left hand when serving wine and use it to wipe the bottle, particularly when taking it out of the ice bucket. Do not wrap the bottle in a towel since the guests usually wish to see the label of the wine they are drinking.

When the host has approved the wine, pour wine: 1) *for a couple*, the lady; 2) *for a group*, the person sitting to the host's right. Proceed around the table counterclockwise, filling the host's glass last. White wine glasses should not be filled more than two thirds full. This gives the drinker an opportunity to savor the wine's aroma within the enclosure of the glass before sipping it.

When pouring wine, hold the bottle so that the label is always uppermost and can readily be seen. Bring the bottle to the glass on the table. Do not lift the glass in your hand because the hand warms the glass and spoils the effect of the chilled white wine. When the glass is two thirds full,
Continued

Steps in opening a wine bottle.

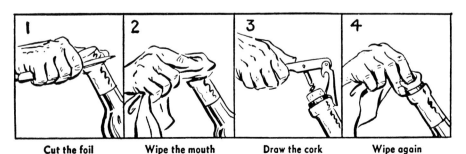

1	2	3	4
Cut the foil	Wipe the mouth	Draw the cork	Wipe again

(**Well below the lip** of the bottle)

Photographs from the collection of Professor Vance A. Christian of Cornell University.

Above — left: The arched entrance with wine bottles stored on either side enhances the wine-cellar atmosphere of the Park Lane Manor restaurant in Buffalo, N.Y. Unusual bottles add to the decor. Right — top: "Wine of the Week" display along with vintner-supplied brochures promotes wine sales at the Manila Inter-Continental Hotel. Right — lower: Wine casks along one dining room wall promote wine sales at the Manila Hilton. Wine drawn from casks should be featured only when sales are high, so that the wine does not deteriorate with age.

Left: Informal restaurants often serve wine in carafes or pitchers, particularly the less expensive wines purchased in bulk. This enables one guest to order a carafe of white wine while another has red or rosé. Two or more people may select a large carafe or pitcher of one wine. The guests fill their own glasses and frequently order another round.

Photograph courtesy of the Waldorf-Astoria.

(*Above*)
This formal dinner, held at the Waldorf-Astoria, features gold service and glasses for six wines.

(*Right*)
Etched, gold-decorated stemware is used at the Waldorf-Astoria for special dinners.

White Wine Glasses: Left — Rhine wine type 8 oz. capacity. Right — tulip 7 oz. capacity. Both contain 4 oz. of wine.

Red Wine Glasses: Left — oversize 23 oz. capacity. Right — 9 oz. capacity. Both contain 4 oz. of wine.

twist the bottle to distribute the last drop on the bottle's rim and thus prevent it from dripping.

When all glasses have been served, place the white wine bottle back into the ice bucket to the host's right. Keep an eye on the table and replenish the guests' glasses when most of them are empty.

How to Serve Red Wines

Red wine is a perfect companion to dark meated fowl, all kinds of meat however prepared, and is excellent with cheese. It is generally served at room temperature. If brought directly from the wine cellar it should be served at that temperature—never warmed. Some lighter bodied red wines may be preferred when slightly chilled, particularly in summer.

Red wine often throws a sediment as it grows older. This is a natural occurrence and shows that the wine is maturing in the bottle. For this reason red wine should be handled carefully and gently. Wine baskets were originally invented to transport old wines from storage to the place where they were decanted prior to serving. Today decanting is rarely required and should not be attempted by anyone but an expert.

Since wine baskets are attractive, many restaurants use them. Pouring wine from a basket is more difficult than pouring from a bottle, and tends to disturb any sediment. Therefore extreme care is required when a basket is used.

Presenting and opening the wine. Red wine should be carefully brought to the table without shaking or turning it, in case there is any sediment. It should be presented to the host for his approval before opening. Again, care should be taken not to disturb any sediment present. When using a wine basket the bottle should be left in the basket during the presenting, opening and serving of the wine. Otherwise, the opening is the same as for white wines.

Place the red wine bottle to the right of the host in a basket as shown, or standing up without the basket, on a mat.

46

Pouring red wines. Red wine glasses are generally larger than white wine glasses and therefore should be filled only one-half to two-thirds full. The serving procedure is the same as for white wine. After filling the glasses, return the bottle to its place at the right side of the host so that he can pour more wine if he desires to do it himself.

How to Serve Champagne

Champagne, the sparkling "king of wines," proper for any occasion, is the most delightful wine obtainable. Champagne can be served with every meal — champagne breakfasts are not unknown — and it can be served before, with all courses, and also after the meal. Sparkling Burgundy and other sparkling wines can be served in much the same fashion as champagne. Champagne must be chilled. The carbon dioxide imprisoned in the wine gives it flavor as well as sparkle.

Before opening champagne. Bring the chilled champagne bottle into the dining room, place it in an ice bucket and set it on a stand to the host's right as you do with white wines. Next, present the unopened bottle to the host for his approval before burying it again in the ice. Place iced champagne glasses (*see this page*) on the table so that the guests can anticipate their pleasure.

Opening the bottle. Because of the pressure inside the bottle, the cork is secured by a wire hood. This safety wire and the foil covering the cork must be removed. Twist the little loop of wire on the bottle neck until it opens; then the wire and foil can be stripped off. While removing the hood, hold the bottle at a 45-degree angle and keep your hand over the cork in case it should pop out itself.

First, wrap the bottle in a napkin and hold it at a 45-degree angle. Grasp the cork firmly and twist the bottle — not the cork. Allow the pressure to force the cork out gently — not with a loud pop. After the cork is out, continue holding the bottle at the 45-degree angle for a few seconds. This will prevent any wine from foaming out of the bottle. Twisting the bottle and not the cork during the opening will prevent broken corks which are difficult to remove. An unprotected champagne cork can be an unpleasant and sometimes dangerous missile. Always protect it from flying out and make sure that the bottle is not pointed at a guest.

Champagne Glasses: Left — saucer 4 oz. capacity 2 1/2 oz. fill. Center — tulip 10 oz. capacity, 4 oz. fill. Right — flute 5 1/2 oz. capacity, 3 oz. fill.

Opening Champagne Bottle

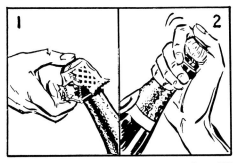

(1) Remove wire and foil in one action. (2) Hold bottle at 45° angle. Grip cork firmly and twist bottle to loosen cork.

(3) As pressure forces cork out, continue to hold it firmly. (4) Pour in two motions, letting foam subside after first pouring.

47

Pouring champagne. Now remove the napkin from the bottle. It was only used to protect you until the bottle was opened and to give you a better grip on the bottle. Serve the host a taste first. On his approval pour the wine in two motions. First pour about one-third of a glass, let the foam subside, and then fill the glass two-thirds to three-quarters full. The balance of service is the same as for white wine.

Some Beverage Suggestions with Various Foods

Apertif and dessert wines are served in the manner of cocktails and other mixed drinks. These wines are ordered at the bar and brought into the dining room on a small bar tray. Each glass is then set before the guest.

• *Before dinner or with the appetizers*: cocktails, highballs, sherry, apertif wines, madeira, vermouth. Sherry and aperitif wines are often served "on the rocks" in a short-stemmed bar glass. Nowadays a dry white wine or a "Kir" (white wine and Crême de Cassis) are becoming popular appetizers.

• *With fish or fowl*: dry and medium-dry white table wines, rosé (pink) wines.

• *With steaks, roasts and other meats*: red table wines.

• *With dessert*: champagne, sparkling wines, sweet white **table wines.**

A display cart of liqueur bottles and glasses promotes the sale of after-dinner drinks.

• *With cheese*: red table wines, port.

• *After dinner*: liqueurs or brandy.

• *With all courses*: champagne.

Banquet Setting: Red wine glass to the left, white wine glass to the right, sherry in front.

48

9. Glassware

Knowledge of the names and appearances of the most-used glasses is necessary for the waiter to provide proper wine service. The two major glass types are *cylindrical* (resembling the ordinary water glass) and *stemmed* (derived from the goblet of olden days).

Manufacturers of glassware are constantly introducing new designs, shapes, and content to their glasses. The appearance of those offered by different manufacturers differ for the same type of glass. However, for general use in wine service for the small restaurant, an all-purpose wine glass may be sufficient. This glass should be stemmed, have a tulip shape, and a generous capacity of 6 to 10 ounces.

Placement of Wine Glasses

Table setting requires correct placement of wine glasses. Wine glasses are set to the right of the plate and towards the center of the table. *When three wines are to be served, set one wine glass in line with knife, one to the right and one below it, forming a triangle.* Glasses may also be set in a straight line in front of and to the right of place — the water goblet and the wine glasses in that order.

Banquet wine service usually progresses from the lighter dry wines, often the white wines served with appetizers and the fish course, to the full-bodied red wines served with beef or game.

(Sherry may accompany certain soups.) With dessert, champagne or a sweet wine may be offered. This order indicates the placement of appropriate glasses on the table, with the glass for the first wine to be served in the outer position. After-dinner liqueurs, when offered with coffee, may be served from a cart which holds suitable glasses. If several wines are served the glasses are removed when the course with which they are served is finished.

Bar Glasses

Bar glasses are growing larger and more decorative for several reasons. Mixed drinks are increasingly being ordered "on the rocks," which requires a larger glass than the standard cocktail. More establishments are featuring a king-size 1.5 oz. drink at a higher price than the standard cocktail, which in communities that have a one-drink ritual increases the bar sales. Less labor and glassware are needed for the one large drink than if two standard cocktails are sold. The decanter and often the bottom of the shaker can be eliminated when large glasses are used. Finally, the large drink in an ornamental glass appeals to customers.

Shown at the bottom of this page are the commonly used bar glasses which are being superseded in many places by larger and more decorative glasses. For instance, a Bloody Mary or Collins-type drink may be served on the rocks in a

(*Right*)
Typical Bar Glasses: (Left to right) Top row — collins, brandy snifter, Delmonico (whisky sour), cocktail. Center row — highball, liqueur, sherry, champagne saucer. Bottom row — old fashioned (on the rocks), small snifter, cocktail decanter, shot.

(*Above*)
Specially designed bar glasses used by the Bull & Bear restaurant of the Waldorf-Astoria: (Left to right) beer shell or Collins, highball, water, sour, old fashioned, cocktail, sherry, shot.

14 to 16 oz. tumbler with a straw. A variation of the Whisky Sour may be served on the rocks in a pilsner glass. And the Manhattan or Martini may be served on the rocks in a 5 to 6 oz. short-stemmed goblet.

In Polynesian restaurants, the serving glass may be more exotic than the drink — real and simulated coconut shell, decorative pottery mugs, tall glasses of serpentine shape, bowls holding drinks for two or four persons, fresh pineapple shells.

Types of Glasses. A few of the more commonly used bar glasses are described below:

Champagne: The most common type is the "saucer" which holds 4 to 5 oz. The tulip-shaped and the flute glass are becoming more and more popular since they show off the bubbles better and hold the sparkle longer.

Wine: These glasses come in many styles and may hold from 5 to 10 oz or more. The top and bowl are of medium size and the glass is slightly deeper than wide. Red wine glasses as a rule are larger than white wine glasses. The "all purpose" wine glass is popular because it saves money on inventory and storage space.

Beer Glasses: Left to right — tankard, pilsner, modified pilsner, shell.

NAVY GROG
Powerfully good, laced with stout-hearted Hudson Bay 91⁄4
...a rum to remember
2.50

SCORPION
A smoothie with a pleasant sting
2.95

MISSIONARY'S DOWNFALL
Fresh, crushed mint leaves give this temptress her lovely color
1.95

MAI TAI
The next best thing to a trip to the Islands
2.50

PI YI
As Hawaiian as "Aloha" Including fresh crushed pineapple straight from the Islands
2.75

CHI CHI
"Old Timer" to you... served in a ceramic coconut which is yours to take home
3.50

PLANTER'S RUM PUNCH
Honorable Ancestor to the mixed rum drink
1.95

ZOMBIE
Created at Don the Beachcomber, Hollywood in 1934. Its crowning touch, a tot of the rich rum known as Demerara
2.75

MONTEGO BAY
Will set your sails and box your compass
1.95

DOUBLE SCORPION
(For two or more) A festive presentation fresh gardenias and long straws
5.50

PENANG No. 1
An exotic mixture sparked with passion fruit
2.75

PROUD BIRD
To put you in the Aloha mood!
1.95

BEACH BOY
Coconut milk and vodka – innocent – but watch it!
2.50

FOGCUTTER
Makes everything clear as a bell
2.75

COFFEE GROG
The perfect caper to a Beachcomber dinner
1.95

Polynesian drinks should be served in large, ornamental containers.

Photograph courtesy of Don the Beachcomber.

Cocktail: Like the wine glass, cocktail glasses come in many sizes and shapes. The standard glass has a wide top, shallow bowl, and holds from 3 to 6 oz. However, for cocktails "on the rocks" the 5 to 6 oz. short-stemmed goblet is becoming increasingly popular.

Sour: Used for Whisky Sours, this glass has a narrow top, deep, bowl, parallel sides, and holds 3 to 6 oz. Again, the large "on the rocks" drink served in stemmed goblet or pilsner glass is growing in popularity.

Sherry: This glass has a wide top, slanting side to a deep bowl, and holds 2 to 3 oz. Sherry "on the rocks" is now often served in the 5 to 6 oz. goblet or in an Old Fashioned glass.

Large Brandy Snifter: Often called a "Brandy Inhaler," it resembles in shape an over-sized electric light bulb on a stem and holds 6 to 12 oz. but is actually filled with about 2 ounces of brandy.

Pony: This stemmed, small tubular-shaped glass holds from ¾ to 1 oz. It is dif-ficult to fill and usually the guest gets some of the contents on the outside, thus getting his fingers wet and sticky. This glass is obsolete and is rapidly being replaced by the —

Liqueur glass: A short-stemmed, n a r r o w tulip-shaped glass holds 3 oz. with or without a line at the 1 oz. level.

Tom Collins: This large cylindrical glass resembles an ordinary water glass and usually holds 12 oz.

Highball: Smaller than Tom Collins but the same shape, this glass holds 5 to 10 oz.

Old Fashioned: Short, squat glass that is wider at top than bottom and holds 4 to 10 oz. These drinks, however, are often served in a more ornamental glass.

Double-Size Bar (or Shot): The same shape as the Old Fashioned but smaller, this glass holds about 2 oz.

Bull Shot: Bouillon with whisky is served in the Old Fashioned glass or "on the rocks" in a larger goblet-style glass.

Large wine glasses can be used for cocktails, apertif wines, fruit cups, desserts, and even to hold small table bouquets.

This wine basket holding a decanter and four glasses simplifies table service in the informal restaurant. A table tent card might sell both wine and the baskets, which also come in a size to hold six glasses.

APPENDIX

Dining Room Service Check

The check list given below may be used by "special guests" checking on service at the request of management or circulated among selected patrons at periodic intervals. Ideally, the staff should not be aware that a check is being made so that the rating will be upon "normal" service. The completed form can be used in staff briefing sessions.

Date   Time entered: Time service completed:

Number of persons in party: Your check No. (*from stub*)_____

In what dining area were you: Waiter's No. (*from stub*) _____

Your Host (or Hostess):

Did anyone greet you?   Yes ☐   No ☐

Did the greeting seem: (*Check appropriate words.*)

_____Courteous?   _____Routine?

_____Friendly?   _____Lacking in spirit?

_____Sincere?   _____Indifferent?

Did you make a reservation?   Yes ☐   No ☐

Were you kept waiting for a table?   Yes ☐   No ☐

Did you like the table (location) you were assigned?   Yes ☐   No ☐

Did the host assist you in seating yourself (party)?   Yes ☐   No ☐

Leave the table abruptly?   Yes ☐   No ☐

Hover about a bit?   Yes ☐   No ☐

Return to your table or area to survey service?   Yes ☐   No ☐

Was the manner of the host (*Check appropriate words*):

       _____Gracious?   _____Bored?

       _____Discourteous?   _____Did he smile?

Did he make any comment?   Yes ☐   No ☐

If so, was his voice: (*Check proper word*)

             _____Pleasing and clear?

             _____Difficult to hear?

             _____Harsh or too loud?

Any comment about the host?

Posture and general appearance: _____Good   _____Fair   _____Poor

Personal: _____Hair neat?   _____Clothing neat and

             _____Shoes trim?   appropriate?

       Other comments:

CASHIER'S RECORD

FORM 5   Cashier_____   Date_____

Waitress No. 1				Waitress No. 2				Waitress No. 3				Waitress No. 4				No. 21		CHARGE						SUMMARY		
Check No.	No. Per.	Amt.	√	Check No.	No. Per.	Amt.	√	Check No.	No. Per.	Amt.	√	Check No.	No. Per.	Amt.	√	Amt.	√	Check No.	Wait No.	No. Per.	Room No.	NAME OF GUEST	Amt.	Wait No.	No. Per.	Cash	Charge

Record form to keep waiters' performance separately.

54

Your Waiter or Waitress: (*Check appropriate words*)

Voice: ____Clear and pleasing   Manner: ____Courteous
       ____Difficult to hear   ____Indifferent
       ____Harsh or too loud   ____Flippant

Were you served: ____Quietly and efficiently?   ____Awkwardly?
                   ____Carelessly?   ____Too slowly?

Time: Order was taken within____minutes after you were seated.
       Food was served within____minutes after your order was taken.
       Did your waiter repeat your order to you?   Yes ☐ No ☐
       Was the food served as you ordered it?   Yes ☐ No ☐
       If you requested substitutes, did he handle
       them easily?   Yes ☐ No ☐
       Was the dessert order taken and served promptly? Yes ☐ No ☐
       Was your check   ____legible?
                       ____correct?
                       ____given promptly?

Service:
        Did the waiter greet you?   Yes ☐ No ☐
        Offer suggestions?   Yes ☐ No ☐
        Was your water glass refilled?   Yes ☐ No ☐
        Were you offered more rolls?   Yes ☐ No ☐
        Have to ask for added silver?   Yes ☐ No ☐
        Did he offer a final greeting?   Yes ☐ No ☐
        Was his grammar   ____Satisfactory?   ____Poor?

Posture and general appearance: ____Good   ____Fair   ____Poor
Hair neat?   Yes ☐ No ☐   Uniform neat?   Yes ☐ No ☐

Waitress:
Hair net worn?   Yes ☐ No ☐   Excessive perfume?   Yes ☐ No ☐
Apron neatly tied? Yes ☐ No ☐   Excessive makeup?   Yes ☐ No ☐
White shoes clean and in good condition   Yes ☐ No ☐
Jewelry other than wristwatch and ring?   Yes ☐ No ☐

Waiter:
Hair short and neat? Yes ☐ No ☐   Tie neatly tied?   Yes ☐ No ☐
Jacket neat and clean? Yes ☐ No ☐   Trousers pressed?   Yes ☐ No ☐
Collar neat and clean? Yes ☐ No ☐   Shoes neatly shined? Yes ☐ No ☐

Atmosphere
Was dining room: ____Wet or dirty   ____Littered   ____Clean
Temperature and ventilation: ____Good   ____Fair   ____Bad
Was there unnecessary noise in handling dishes?   Yes ☐ No ☐
     ____From "behind the scenes."   ____In the dining room?
Was your table clean?   Yes ☐ No ☐
Items on it neatly arranged?   Yes ☐ No ☐
Was the music: ____Too loud   ____Too soft   ____Agreeable to you?
Other Comments:

General
Were china, glassware and silverware thoroughly clean?   Yes ☐ No ☐
Was the general atmosphere attractive to you?   Yes ☐ No ☐
Was the general appearance of the personnel   ____Good   ____Fair   ____Poor
Remarks on service:

Anything outstanding (good or bad):

Remarks of nearby guests:

Miscellaneous comments:

French Menu Terms

French Term	Definition	Pronunciation
Agneau	Lamb	*ahn-yo*
Aigre	Sour	*aygr*
Ail	Garlic	*eye*
Aileron	Wingbone	*ay-luh-rawn*
Allumette	Match stick potatoes	*ah-loo-met*
Alsacienne	Alsatian style; usually served with saur-kraut	*ahl-sah-seeyan*
Amandine	With almonds	*ah-mawn-deen*
Américaine	American style	*ah-mair-ee-ken*
Ananas	Pineapple	*ah-nah-nah*
Anchois	Anchovy	*awn-schwah*
Andalouse	With tomatoes & peppers	*awn-dah-loos*
Auguille	Eel	*awn-ghee*
Argenteuil	With asparagus	*ahr-zhawn-toy*
Artichaut	Artichoke	*ahr-tee-show*
Asperges	Asparagus	*ah-spayrge*
Aspic	Decorated jellied piece	*ah-speek*
Aubergines	Egg Plant	*oh-bare-zheen*
Bèarnaise	In America, a sauce similar to hollandaise, fortified with meat glaze, and with tarragon flavor predominating	*bair-nez*
Bécasse	Woodcock	*bay-khace*
Béchamel	Cream sauce	*bay-shaw-mel*
Beignet	Fritter	*bayn-yay*
Beurre	Butter	*burr*
Bifteck	Beefsteak	*bif-teck*
Bisque	Thick, rich soup	*beesk*
Blanc	White	*blawnk*
Blanquette	Stew with white wine	*blawn-ket*
Boeuf	Beef	*buff*
Boisson	Drink, Beverage	*bawh-sawn*
Bouillabaisse	Fish stew	*bwee-yuh-baze*
Bouillon	Broth	*bwee-yawn*
Bouquetière	With mixed vegetables	*boo-ket-yer*
Bourguignonne	With onions and red Burgundy wine	*boor-geen-yawn*
Bouteille	Bottle	*boo-tie*
Café	Coffee	*kah-fay*
Canard	Duck	*kah-nahr*
Caneton	Duckling	*kah-nuh-tawn*
Carré	Rack	*kah-ray*
Cervelle	Brain	*sir-vel*
Champignon	Mushroom	*shawn-peen-yawn*
Chapon	Capon	*shah-pawn*
Chateaubriand	Thick Filet Mignon	*shah-to-bree-yawn*
Chaud	Warm, Hot	*show*
Chevreuil	Venison	*shuv-roy*
Chou-Fleur	Cauliflower	*shoo-flure*
Choux de Bruxelles	Brussel sprouts	*shoo-duh-brewzel*
Cochon	Suckling pig	*ko-shawn*
Coeur	Heart	*koor*
Compote	Stewed fruit	*kawn-pawt*
Concombre	Cucumber	*kawn-kawmbr*
Confiture	Jam, preserve	*kawn-fee-toor*
Consommé	Clear soup	*kawn-saw-may*
Coquille	Shell for baking	*ko-kee*
Cote	Rib, Chop	*kaw*
Crème	Cream	*krem*
Crème Fouettée	Whipped cream	*krem-fo-et-tay*
Crêpe	Pancake	*krepp*
Crevette	Shrimp	*kruh-vet*
Croquette	Patty of meat	*kro-ket*
Déjeuner	Breakfast, Lunch	*day-zhoo-nay*
Diable	Deviled	*dee-abl*
Dinde	Turkey	*dand*
Du Barry	With cauliflower	*du-bahree*
Eau	Water	*oh*
Ecrevisse	Crayfish	*ay-kruh-veece*
Entrecote	Sirloin steak	*awn-truh-kawt*
Entremets	Sweet, Desserts	*awn-truh-meh*
Epinard	Spinach	*ay-pee-nahr*
Escargots	Snails	*es-kahr-go*
Faisan	Pheasant	*fay-zawn*
Farce	Ground meat	*fahrce*
Farci	Stuffed	*fahr-see*
Filet	Boneless ribbon	*fee-lay*
Flambé	Flamed	*flawn-bay*
Foie	Liver	*fwah*
Foie Gras	Goose liver	*fwah-grah*
Fondue	Melted cheese	*fawn-doo*
Forestière	With mushroom	*faw-rest-teeyer*
Four	Oven baked	*foor*
Fricandeau	Braised veal morsels	*free-kahn-doe*
Fricassée	Chicken or veal stew	*free-kah-say*
Frit	Deep fat fried	*free*
Froid	Cold	*frwah*
Fromage	Cheese	*froh-mahge*
Fumé	Smoked	*foo-may*
Gateau	Cake	*gah-toe*
Gelée	Jelly	*zhuh-lay*
Gibier	Game	*zhee-bee-yay*
Gigot	Leg	*zhee-go*
Glacé	Ice, ice cream	*glah-say*
Gratin	Brown, baked with cheese	*grah-tan*
Grenouille	Frog	*gruh-noo-ee*
Grillé	Broiled	*gree-yay*
Hereng	Herring	*ah-rawng*
Haricot Vert	String beans	*ah-ree-ko-ver*
Hollandaise	Sauce made with egg yolk, melted butter, and lemon	*aw-lawn-dez*
Homard	Lobster	*oh-mar*
Hors d'Oeuvres	Pre-dinner tidbits	*or-durve*
Huitre	Oyster	*wheatr*
Jambon	Ham	*zhahn-bawn*
Jardinière	With vegetable	*zhahr-dan-yer*
Julienne	Thin strips	*zhool-yen*
Jus	Juice, gravy	*zhoo*
Lait	Milk	*lay*
Langouste	Sea crayfish or rock lobster	*lawn-goost*
Lapin	Rabbit	*lah-pan*
Légume	Vegetable	*lay-goom*
Macédoine	Mixed fruits	*mah-suh-dwahn*
Maître d'Hotel	With spiced butter	*maytr-doe-tell*
Marmite	Pot; Stew	*mahr-meet*
Meringue	Beaten egg white	*meh-rang*
Meunière	Pan fried and served with brown butter	*moon-yer*
Mignon	Dainty	*mee-yawn*
Mornay	Cheese sauce	*mor-nay*
Mousse	Whipped foam	*moose*
Mouton	Mutton	*moo-tawn*
Nantua	Lobster sauce	*nahn-too-ah*
Naturel	Plain	*nah-tew-rel*
Noir	Black	*nwah*
Noisette	Hazelnut	*swah-zet*
Nouille	Noodle	*noo-ee*

French Term	Definition	Pronunciation	French Term	Definition	Pronunciation
Oeuf	Egg	uf	Riz	Rice	ree
Oeufs Pochés	Poached eggs	uf-paw-shay	Rognon	Kidney	rawn-yawn
Oie	Goose	wah	Roti	Roasted	ro-tee
Oignon	Onion	awn-yawn	Roulade	Rolled meat	roo-lahd
Pain	Bread	pan	Saumon	Salmon	saw-mone
Paté	Meat pie	pah-tay	Sauté	Pan fried in butter	saw-tay
Patisserie	Pastry	pah-tee-suh-ree	Sel	Salt	sell
Pêche	Peach	pesh	Selle	Saddle	sell
Petit	Small	puh-tee	Sorbet	Sherbet	sawr-bay
Poire	Pear	pwahr	Soufflé	Whipped pudding	soo-flay
Pois	Peas	pwah	Tasse	Cup	tahce
Poisson	Fish	pwah-sawn	Tête	Head	tet
Poitrine	Breast	pwah-treen	Tournedos	Two small tenderloin steaks	toor-nuh-do
Pomme	Apple	pawn			
Pomme de Terre	Potato	pawn-duh-ter	Tranche	Slice	trawnsh
Potage	Soup	poh-tahge	Truite	Trout	trew-eet
Pot Au Feu	Boiled beef with a variety of vegetables and broth served as a meal	paw-toe-foo	Veau	Veal	vo
			Veloute	White sauce made from fish, chicken, or veal stock	vuh-lootay
Poulet	Chicken	poo-lay	Vichyssoise	Hot or cold potato and leek soup	vee-shee-swahz
Purée	Sieved food	poo-ray			
Quenelle	Dumpling	kuh-nel	Viennoise	Vienna style, breaded	vee-yen-wahz
			Vinaigrette	Dressing with oil, vinegar and herbs	vee-nay-gret
Ragout	Stew	rah-goo	Volaille	Poultry	vo-lie
Ris	Sweetbread	ree	Vol au Vent	Patty shell	vole-oh-vawn

Audio-Visual Training Aids

For information on some audio-visual training aids currently available, write to National Educational Media, 15760 Ventura Boulevard, Encino, CA 91436.

The National Restaurant Association (One IBM Plaza, Suite 2600, Chicago, IL 60611), the National Institute for the Foodservice Industry (20 North Wacker Drive, Chicago, IL 60606), the American Hotel & Motel Association (888 Seventh Avenue, New York, NY 10019), and the Council on Hotel, Restaurant, and Institutional Education (Henderson Human Development Building, Pennsylvania State University, University Park, PA 16802) are other good sources of information on training materials.

Many food, beverage, and equipment manufacturers and suppliers (e.g., distillers, wineries) also provide training films, many at no charge.

Table Service Arrangements

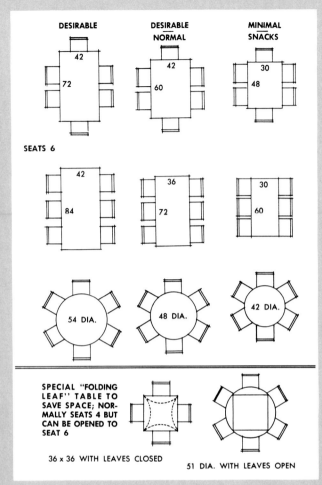

SEATS 6

SPECIAL "FOLDING LEAF" TABLE TO SAVE SPACE; NORMALLY SEATS 4 BUT CAN BE OPENED TO SEAT 6

36 x 36 WITH LEAVES CLOSED

51 DIA. WITH LEAVES OPEN

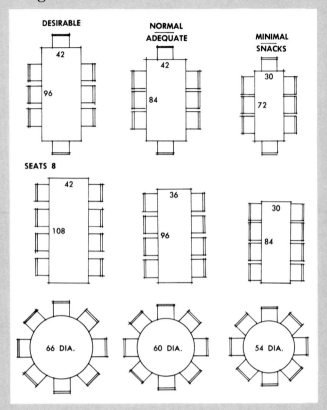

SEATS 8

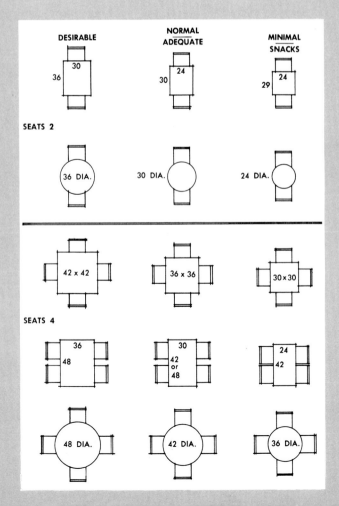

SEATS 2

SEATS 4

All of these figures are meant to serve only as guides—only your designer or booth or table manufacturer can give you a plan that you can depend upon to give you the best possible dining arrangement for your particular needs.

Drawings are divided into two categories:

1. Table Service Dining
   a. Desirable to give most comfortable dining
   b. Normal or adequate
   c. Minimal not for full meals adequate only for snacks or cocktails
2. Cafeteria Dining (with trays)
   a. 14 x 18 standard rectangular tray
   b. 15 x 22 "Spacesaver" tray triangular shape

Drawings are scaled $\frac{1}{8}$" = 1'0".

—All drawings are shown with an 18" wide side chair. If arm chairs (24" wide) are used additional room must be allowed—also make sure the arm will go underneath the table top.

—Basic rule of thumb for table dining—each place setting should be approximately 24"w x 15"d, with additional room allowed for condiments.

—Table height for normal dining is 29" or 30". Chair seat height for normal dining is 17" or 18".

—From chair back to chair back: 36" minimum; 24" minimum.

—Aisles: Public circulation service *only*. (Chair in use will normally extend 15" beyond table edge)

—To figure seating capacity:
   Take square footage of table area.
   Divide by: 10 sq. ft. for banquet seating or snacks
   12 sq. ft. for cafeteria or normal dining
   15 sq. ft. for desirable uncrowded dining

These figures do not allow for unusual room conditions such as columns, numerous doorways or unusual architectural features—wall jogs, etc.

Courtesy of *Cooking for Profit* magazine.

NAPKIN FOLDING

THE TENT

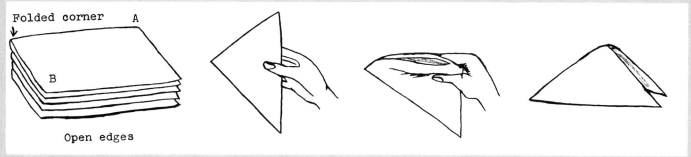

This simple fold can be done with one hand while the other carries the napkin stack. Place stack of folded square napkins in left hand, with the folded corner above the left thumb. With the right thumb, fold corner A down to corner B, as shown in the second diagram, and then curl this triangle around the thumb to form a "tent." Tent napkins can be positioned on the table as shown, or with either the open or closed end facing the guest.

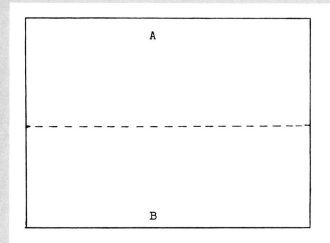

THE COCKED HAT
(See page 14.)

This napkin fold is very simple to do and the folded napkins can be stacked.

Fold rectangular napkin into halves and crease. Next fold the right-hand third toward the napkin's middle and crease. Roll C down to within 1-1/2" of napkin edges A-B with your right hand and then turn D over it with your left. Turn up point E and then F with your thumbs as shown in the diagram.

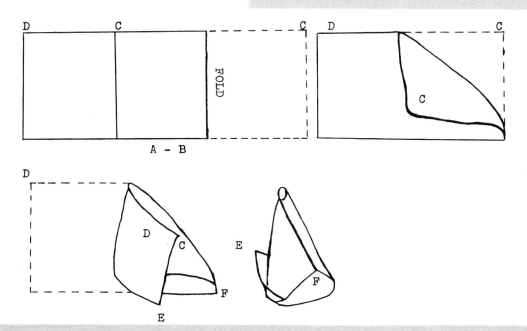

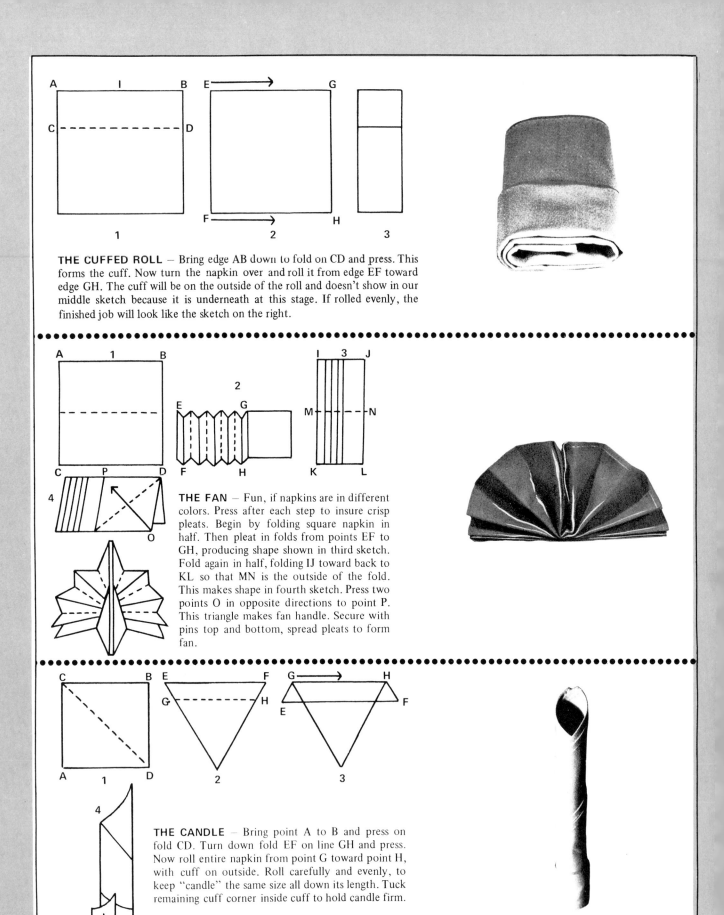

THE CUFFED ROLL — Bring edge AB down to fold on CD and press. This forms the cuff. Now turn the napkin over and roll it from edge EF toward edge GH. The cuff will be on the outside of the roll and doesn't show in our middle sketch because it is underneath at this stage. If rolled evenly, the finished job will look like the sketch on the right.

THE FAN — Fun, if napkins are in different colors. Press after each step to insure crisp pleats. Begin by folding square napkin in half. Then pleat in folds from points EF to GH, producing shape shown in third sketch. Fold again in half, folding IJ toward back to KL so that MN is the outside of the fold. This makes shape in fourth sketch. Press two points O in opposite directions to point P. This triangle makes fan handle. Secure with pins top and bottom, spread pleats to form fan.

THE CANDLE — Bring point A to B and press on fold CD. Turn down fold EF on line GH and press. Now roll entire napkin from point G toward point H, with cuff on outside. Roll carefully and evenly, to keep "candle" the same size all down its length. Tuck remaining cuff corner inside cuff to hold candle firm.

Courtesy of *Hospitality magazine*

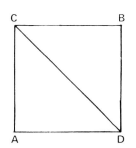

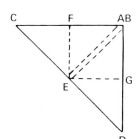

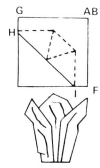

CARDINAL'S HAT IN WINE GLASS — This is folded the same as regular Cardinal's Hat, but, instead of tucking corners H and I together, roll corner H back and fold corner I behind H to form roll which will fit into wine glass. Use a red napkin to suggest service of wine with the meal.

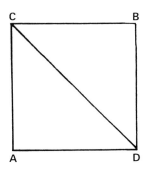

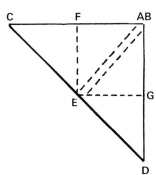

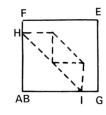

THE SHRINE — Bring point A to B and press along line C-D. Then fold corners C and D to point AB. Now turn napkin to opposite side, reversing points AB and E. Fold point AB to approximately 3/4 of the way up to point E and back down to line H-I. Bring corners H and L together, tucking one into the other, forming a round base. Stand the napkin up and flair out top center to form shrine.

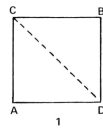

1

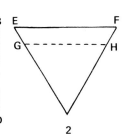

2

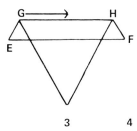

3

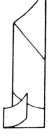

4

CANDLE IN WINE GLASS — This is folded the same as in directions for folding the candle. Use a red napkin and place in wine glass to suggest service of wine with the meal.

Courtesy of *Hospitality magazine*

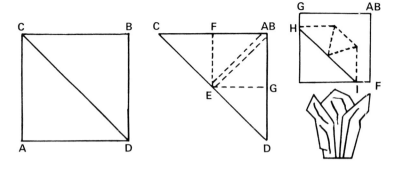

CARDINAL'S HAT — Bring point A to B and press along line C-D. Then fold corners C and D to point AB. Now turn napkin to opposite side, reversing points F and G. Fold point E approximately 3/4 of way up to point AB and back down to line HI. Bring corners H and I together, tucking one into the other, forming a round base. Stand the napkin up and flair out points slightly.

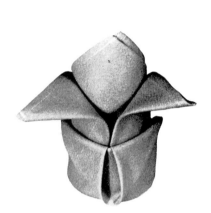

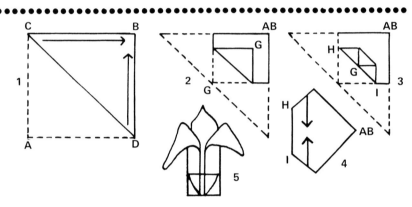

THE CROWN — Bring point A to B and press along line CD. Then fold corners C & D to point AB. Now bring point G approximately 2/3 of the way up to AB and press, as shown in Sketch No. 2. Now bring point G back to line HI, as shown in Sketch No. 3. Turn napkins to opposite side, as in Sketch No. 4. Bring corners H and I together, tucking one into the other, thus forming a round base. Stand the napkin up and flair out the two top corners, forming the crown.

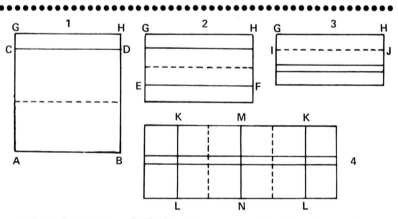

THE TRIPLE TIER — Fold edge AB up to meet line CD and press. Next, bring same edge AB down to new line EF and press again. Now bring top edge GH down to line IJ, just slightly overlapping the down fold already made. Now, at line KL, fold the two ends under, then bring folds KL to meet at the center line MN.

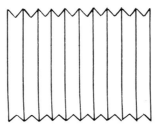

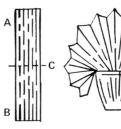

WATER GLASS FAN — Fold napkin complete width in accordion folds. Fold in half and press tightly. Push folded point C into water glass. Clip or pin inside folds A and B together at top and let sides fall over glass to form fan.

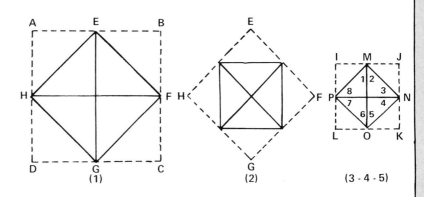

THE ROSE — CENTERPIECE — Steps 1 and 2 are to fold all corners ABCD to center, then fold points EFGH to center. Turn napkin to opposite side. Step 3, fold all corners IJKL to center. Make sure that all folds to this point are pressed tightly. Step 4, place two fingers of left hand at points 1 and 2, halfway between center and point M. Reach under point M and grasp flap (holding down firmly with fingers) and pull flap straight up. Repeat this operation at points N, O and P. Step 5, place two fingers of left hand at points 2 and 3, halfway between center and side MN. Reach under side MN and grasp flap (holding down firmly with fingers) and pull flap straight up. Repeat this operation with sides NO, OP and PM.

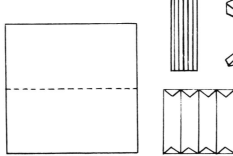

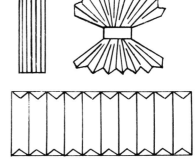

RING FAN — Fold napkin in half. Starting from one end of half-folded napkin, fold in accordion folds the complete length, pressing folds in firmly. Using a split plastic ring, place ring in center of folds with folded edges up. Spread ends out as in diagram.

Courtesy of *Hospitality magazine*

HOW TO CARVE BEEF AND HAM

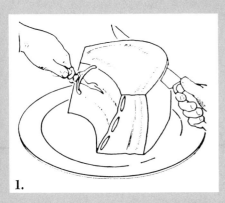 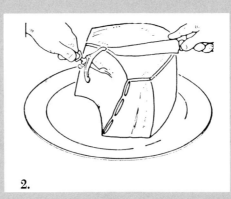 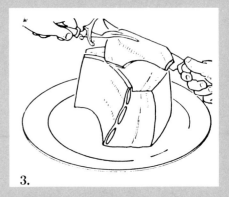

STANDING RIB ROAST OF BEEF

1. Place the roast on the platter with the largest end down to form a solid base. Insert the fork between the two top ribs. Starting on the fat side, carve across the grain to the rib bone.

2. Use the tip of the knife to cut along the rib bone to loosen the slice. Be sure to keep close to the bone to make the largest servings possible.

3. Slide the knife back under the slice and, steadying it with the fork, lift the slice to the side of the platter. If the platter is not large enough, place the slices on a heated platter close by.

Steamship Round of Beef

Place roast shank-side down on a cutting board and carve from the top. Customers will first receive cuts from the top round, bottom round, rump, and sirloin tip. Make thin horizontal slices across the muscle structure toward the bone. Cut slices evenly from all sides of the roast to prevent shredding.

BAKED WHOLE HAM

1. Place the ham on the platter with the decorated side up and the shank to the carver's right. Remove several slices from the ham's thin side to form a solid base on which to set the ham.

2. Turn the ham on its base. Starting at the shank end, cut and remove a small wedge. Then carve perpendicular to the leg bone as shown in the diagram.

3. Release slices by cutting under them and along the leg bone, starting at the shank end. For additional servings, turn ham over to the original position and make slices to the bone, release and serve.

 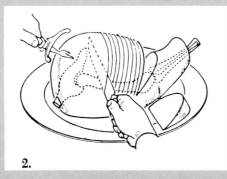 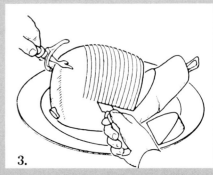

Courtesy of the National Livestock Board

HOW TO CARVE A TURKEY

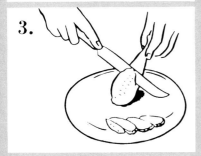

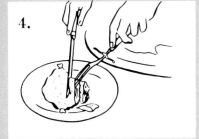

1. Remove the leg (thigh and drumstick) by holding the leg firmly with your fingers and pulling it gently away from the turkey as you cut through the front skin between the leg and body.

2. Then cut through the joint between the leg and backbone at the back of the carcass. Hold the leg on a service plate and separate the thigh from the drumstick by cutting down through the joint.

3. To slice drumstick meat, hold the drumstick upright at an angle to the plate and cut down, turning the drumstick to get uniform slices.

4. To slice the thigh, hold it firmly on the plate with a fork and cut slices of meat parallel to the bone.

5. Make a deep horizontal cut into the turkey breast, parallel to the body frame, starting close to the wing. (The wings of large turkeys are removed before roasting.)

6. To slice white meat, start half way up the breast, cutting thin slices of white meat down to the parallel cut. The slices will fall away neatly if cut down to this line.

Courtesy of the Poultry and Egg National Board

Decorative Ice Carving

Harry C. Gibbons, Jr., Director of Dietary Services, Christ Hospital, Cincinnati

An illuminated ice carving adds glamour to the decoration of a buffet table and is surprisingly easy to sculpture. All that is needed, other than the desire to carve something, is a large block of ice, a freezer big enough to hold it between carving sessions, and a one-inch wood chisel.

The maximum-size block of ice readily available weighs 300 lbs. and measures 11 inches in thickness, 22 inches in width, and 42 inches in length. In ordering the block from a local ice company or brewery, be sure to specify that you want an unscored block as it comes from the mold; otherwise it will be saw-marked into 50-lb. blocks. Ask that ice handlers use tongs only at the top corners to avoid making deep dents into the block's soft, opaque center. When delivered, have the ice block placed in the position you want the finished carving — flat or on an edge — on a cart covered with freezer paper to keep the ice from sticking to the cart between carving sessions. Wheel the cart into the freezer.

In carving ice, keep its characteristics in mind: 1) don't try to carve any block which has been dropped, toned hard, or otherwise abused; 2) as a crystalline substance, ice fractures along fairly definite planes without showing visible evidence; 3) don't use a pick to rough out or divide a block because the small rythmic blows may fracture a wide area of ice.

Carving is done at room temperature. The ice block must be frozen hard so that you can control the depth of the wooden chisel. After about 30 minutes at room temperature, the ice block softens so that it is difficult to control the depth of the chisel stroke. Return it to the freezer for several hours to harden before resuming your carving. An exploratory touch with your chisel will tell you when it is hard enough.

Patterns. For your first project, a punch bowl is easy, but such nautical objects as an anchor, fish, or tugboat are also simple to do. First, make your pattern on graph paper and then transfer it to scale on a large piece of freezer paper. A child's coloring book is a rich source for simple drawings. Trace the design you want and use an opaque projector to enlarge it on freezer paper taped to a wall so that you can trace the outline. Or use a toy, stuffed animal, or sculpture which you can photograph and then enlarge. For your design, add a bit of motion — have the fish riding the crest of a wave, have the Easter bunny flop one ear, or the punch bowl become a fountain by means of a tube hooked to a small pump. Above all, don't be too ambitious at first. Success gives you the courage for more intricate carvings.

Tools. Other than the straight one-inch wooden chisel, few other tools are needed. Some experts use a coarse-toothed saw to cut off major unwanted portions, a six-pronged ice shaver, a pick, a V-shaped and a rounded chisel once in a while, but the wooden chisel is usually adequate. An insulated rubberized glove keeps your carving hand protected from melting ice shavings.

Punchbowl. Order a 150-lb., unscored ice block measuring 11 x 22 x 21 inches and have it laid flat on a cart covered with freezer paper. (Make a profile drawing of your bowl to scale.) To outline the top of the bowl, place an 18-in. diameter pot on top to melt in the circle. Or attach a cord to two pointed objects, placing one point at the ice block's center and using the other to trace in the 18-in. diameter circle (a 9 in. measurement from the center). Turn over the ice block and from the carefully ascertained center point, trace a 9-in. diameter circle for the bowl's bottom. (*See Bowl diagrams.*) Working carefully from your drawing, use your chisel to shave off — don't slash or jab — the block's corners to control separation of the ice chunks. Continue until you've shaped a rough hemisphere.

Refreeze your ice block if it begins to soften. Next, from the edge of the bowl bottom use a string to score the bowl first into halves, then quarters, and finally eighths. Use your chisel's edge to make small V-shaped grooves along these scores. Starting at the base of the bowl, round off the eight segments so that they are symmetrical. Turn the bowl upright and return to the freezer to harden. Hollow the bowl by shaving toward the center from a 3-in. rim — resisting the temptation to hurry which may split the bowl. Don't use the rim for leverage, don't try to pry out ice chunks. Some people use a bowl of hot water to melt the center, but this too can be hazardous and messy. Return to the freezer until needed.

For use at receptions, pre-chill the punch almost to the freezing point and place a catch-basin, topped with greenery, under the ice bowl. When the bowl is lighted, the colored punch seen through the crystal-clear ice takes on added glamour. Remember to empty the catch-basin and keep an eye on flaws in the bowl so that the punch doesn't melt through. Two ice bowls, used alternately, may be desirable. Bowls in good shape can be refrozen for later use.

Dolphin. Order a 300-lb. ice block and lay it on a lengthwise edge on freezer paper. Make profile patterns of your dolphin to scale — top and side (*see illustration under "patterns"*). For the side, wet the diagram and let it freeze to the ice. Chisel the pattern outline about one inch outside the edge of external pattern lines and directly over all internal pattern lines. Use a chisel or saw to remove the ice outside

Continued on page 68.

Punch Bowl

(See instructions on the facing page.)

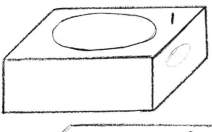

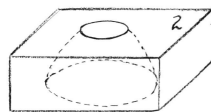

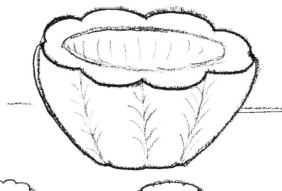

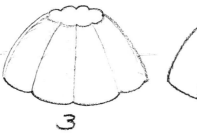

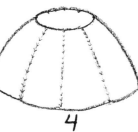

Dolphin

(See instructions on the facing page.
Steps 1, 2, and 3 are shown below.)

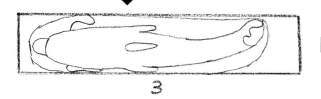

3

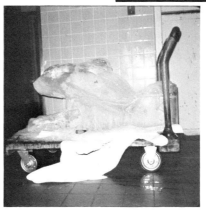

the chiseled outline until you have a profile cutout. (*See Dolphin — steps 1 and 2.*) Refrigerate.

With the top-view pattern before you (*Figure 3*), mark the outline of the dolphin's vertical planes on the ice. (*Lay pattern on the ice if this is helpful.*) Be careful, as you carve vertically, not to cut off the flippers or the top of the wave. Keep checking your side markings. Using a planing, shaving motion with the chisel, round off the square outlines. Carve all over the block — don't try to make the entire head or tail emerge. Refrigerate.

Pull the cart holding the roughly chiseled dolphin to an area with plenty of working space. View it from all angles. Complete your dolphin by chiseling away ice to give it motion, fluidity, and grace. Add eye sockets, small scoring, etc. Remember that you are working with ice, not marble, and that intricate scorings will soon melt.

A large carving like a dolphin needs two 75-watt bulbs spaced beneath it for good illumination. The dophin will last four hours at average room temperature and melt about 6 to 8 gallons of water into a catch basin. When removing the dolphin from the table, use extreme care so that it doesn't skid and fall — it will be slippery and there are no handholds. Massive ice sculptures can be retouched after refrigeration for use several times.

INDEX